D0280633

COLLECTED POEMS: 2

Peter Reading: Collected Poems

1: POEMS 1970-1984 (Bloodaxe Books, 1995)

INTRODUCTION by Isabel Martin
Water and Waste (1970)
For the Municipality's Elderly (1974)
The Prison Cell & Barrel Mystery (1976)
Nothing For Anyone (1977)
Fiction (1979)
Tom o' Bedlam's Beauties (1981)
Diplopic (1983)
5x5x5x5x5 (1983)
C (1984)

2: POEMS 1985-1996 (Bloodaxe Books, 1996)

Ukulele Music (1985)
Going On (1985)
Stet (1986)
Final Demands (1988)
Perduta Gente (1989)
Shitheads (1989)
Evagatory (1992)
Last Poems (1994)
Eschatological (1996)
INDEX OF TITLES AND FIRST LINES

—PETER READING—

Collected Poems

2: POEMS 1985-1996

BLOODAXE BOOKS

ISBN: 1 85224 356 2 hardback edition
1 85224 357 0 paperback edition

First published 1996 by
Bloodaxe Books Ltd,
P.O. Box 1SN,
Newcastle upon Tyne NE99 1SN.

Bloodaxe Books Ltd acknowledges
the financial assistance of Northern Arts.

Cover printing by J. Thomson Colour Printers Ltd, Glasgow.

Printed in Great Britain by
Bell & Bain Limited, Glasgow, Scotland.

To Angela Reading

ACKNOWLEDGEMENTS

The books which comprise volume 2 of Peter Reading's *Collected Poems* were first published as individual collections by the following publishers:

MARTIN SECKER & WARBURG LTD:
Ukulele Music WITH *Going On* (1985)
Stet (1986)
Final Demands (1988)
Perduta Gente (1989)

SQUIRRELPRICK PRESS:
Shitheads (1989)

CHATTO & WINDUS LTD:
Evagatory (1992)
Last Poems (1994)

Some poems from *Ukulele Music* and *Going On* were later republished in *Essential Reading* (Secker & Warburg, 1986). *Ukulele Music* was reprinted as part of *3 in 1* (Chatto & Windus, 1992). 'Prouerbes xiij. iij.', 'Ye haue heard this yarn afore' and 'Gobschighte damapetty'/'Wonderful little Madam' (previously 'Parallel') were first published in *Shitheads*, and were reprinted as part of *Evagatory*, where they appear in this book. Two of the Englished versions of Catullus in *Shitheads* were produced in collusion with M.W.S. Pitter and first appeared in the *Times Literary Supplement*.

The collection *Eschatological* is previously unpublished, and includes poems which first appeared in *Island* (Australia), *Raw Edge*, the *Times Literary Supplement* and the *Sunday Times*.

CONTENTS

UKULELE MUSIC

(1985)

Dear sir,

I come in this morning instead of tomorrow as I have to take ~~Budgie bugdie~~ Bird to the Vets, as he got out of cage door for the first time, By <u>accident</u>. As I was putting seed in. & taking out sand sheet. He went mad. & banged himself against THE wall. & fell down on to the Magic coal fire. got jammed in the back of coal effect. Broken leg and side of his body awfull state. he is in. good job fire was not on.

faithly Viv

p.S. could you oblige the next weeks money this wk. be in tomorrow Morning, Only the Capting which I chars for tuesdays has let me off this Tues but has PAID yrs Viv

Few atrocities
of which H. sap. *can conceive*
remain unfulfilled

'They must have been about 17/18, possibly 19:
one, tattooed on his hand MAM; one, tattooed on his arm LOVE.

One of them grabbed at my handbag but I just belted him with it,
caught him one under the ear, then I yelled "Somebody, help!"

Even although it was lunchtime and several people were watching
nobody wanted to know. Two women just walked right past.'

She had been pushing her 8-month-old, Sharen-Jayne, in the buggy.
Now the kid started to scrawk; one of our heroes smirked, spat,

fondled the empty pint bottle he had in his hand and then smashed it
on an adjacent brick wall, held the bits to the child's throat.

'I said "Hurt me if you like but don't injure the innocent baby –
it can't defend itself, see? Don't do it don't do it *please*!"

He said "If I do the baby I'll get what I want, so I'll cut it."
He shoved the glass in her cheek; twisted the jagged edge in.

He told me "This is how we earn our living, this and the dole like."
Then he just wiggled the sharp, smashed slivers into her eye.'

Promptly the mother gave over her golden wedding-ring, also
three pounds in cash and a watch (silver, engraved 'My True Love'),

but the attackers slashed Sharen twice more – in the mouth, and a deep cut
neatly round one chubby knee. Then they strolled leisurely off.

'Sharen was screaming and bleeding a lot and I thought they had killed her.'
C.I.D. officers say 'This is a callous assault...'

Dear Sir,

will finish of your hoovering and such tomorrow as my hand is still bad, my right one. As last wk. there is a lady two doors off me has a bitch and a little boy over the road had been playing with it. and since then where all the dogs come from I do not know. But one of them had pinned the boy against the wall. I ran out with a handfull of pepper to throw at the dogs face. I throw it. but it had bit me in the hand. just above my right thumb where the bone is. I ran after the dog. with a whitening brush also and I fell also over the fence. bruised my knee's. But my knee is alright. My hand I have sufferd. The dog got put down to sleep. I have been to Hospitle But I heard later. that another dog had pinned the same boy he is only four yrs old. and MARLD him in the face and eyes he has had 5 stitches across his left eye. The other dog also had to be put down to sleep I tell you it has been awfull over there with the dogs. The woman who the bitch belongs to, had forgotten she had left her kitchen window open One of the dogs had jump in through the window. her Husband had delt with the dog. But slammed the kitchen window and all of the glass had fallen out in pieces. (It is awfull. when the little girls are about.) There mothers have to keep them in. or take them with them. the pain is going all the way up my arm. I have had a TECNAS. you know, a little RED CARD.

YRS Viv.

Someone has left a whole crateful of empty lemonade bottles
on the pedestrian bridge. Here come three ten-year-old boys.

Queuing for buses, the off-peak shoppers are gathered together
under the cast concrete span (aerosolled WANKERS and TREV).

Each of the children has picked up an empty and, quite nonchalantly,
hurls it down onto the grans, young mums and spinsters and babes.

No one evinces surprise or alarm or even vexation,
fox-trotting through the smashed bits, Terpsichorean and deft.

Each boy throws four bottles, spits from the parapet into our faces,
shouts 'Fucking bastards' and yelps. Glass crunches under a bus.

Blood smears the calf of an elderly lady silently weeping.
'Kids' our conductor observes 'should be done something about.'

Grans are bewildered by post-Coronation disintegration;
offspring of offspring of *their* offspring infest and despoil.

('You think you're doing a fine job of work don't you, oh yes, but you're not. Stop it stop it, it's dirty dirty dirty in the streets like that' an old woman shopper informs two boys of ten or eleven who slouch against a butcher's window in busy Northcote Rd., SW11. Moist beige tripes gleam. Around the Chopper bikes blobs of bubbly saliva streaked green and yellow describe a semi-circle on the greasy pavement. The boys giggle and one of them remarks sotto voce 'Fuck off old cow'. 'What did you say?' They giggle and do not answer. One boy spits afresh at his colleague's cycle. A glycerite sac depends from the canary-coloured spokes, elongates gradually. 'Dirty little devils. Look at them look at them!' she appeals to those of us nearby. We evince neither surprise nor concern. She turns begrudgingly. Silver streaks jet concurrently from gaps between the front teeth of each boy. She continues upon her way unaware that her pink leatherette mac is sullied by twin viscid drools.)

Stubbornly, Taffs, at their damn-fool anachronistic eisteddfods,
still, with this breach in the hull, twang (ineffectual lyres).

Mercury falls, it's no go, and the pink geraniums shrivel:
ceilidh and Old Viennese drone as the packet goes down.

When all the cities were felled by the pongoid subspecies in them
(Belfast, Jerusalem, Brum., Liverpool, Beirut) and when

blood-swilling (Allah is wonderful) Middle-East Yahoos had purchased
nuclear hardware, he found distich the only form apt.

Too Many Of Us and Dwindled Resources and War had undone us.
Matter impartially throve (quark, strangeness, charm) not as *us*.

Sing in Your Bath if You Want to Seem Sexy and **Blood-Bath**
in Jordan
vie for front page in the tabs. Doh ray me fah soh lah te

well, Sir

Only, the Capting has said I was not really wanted so I have gone to you instead. only. You are not here as you know. So have let myself in with spare key but he has PAY me just the same as he is kind old man with heart of gold etc. and has told me how underneath. and he has seen it with OWN eyes so knows it is true. where I thought it was just Underground Car Park ect. under ~~Civic~~ Civet Centre is not just Car Park but bunk for FALL if there is trouble, that sometimes seems likely with uSA and russiens with there bomb warfair. But what can you do? nothing and he say there are SARDINES stored in there for after siren. with DRINK. so we are all prepared thank God. But what I want to know is when you vote the different Goverments do NOT do what you ask do they? Because I want NO TROUBLE but it seems no difference what you want the Rulers just do a DIFFERENT THING. So you can only keep CHEERFUL and keep trying your best. sir. for Exsample I have done the floors but their is one of Yr writings there that ALAS is swept in the Hoover bag, and I got it out all right but is VERY twisted with the thing that BEATS as SWEEPS as CLEANS the one about a Piano and a Man AND woman that I think is DIRTY but it takes all sorts and did you REALLY work at such a club in uSA? I never knew you had been there but I would not want sardines ALL THE TIME who would? noone. but it would be emergency like in the last one where it was tin sheeting. But now they are on the streets the ARMY against thugs and Mugers as that is where the REAL war is on NOW, cities in 2 halfs with police and army and nice folks against dirty animals, so may HAVE to go DOWN soon for THAT war. But I have throw it away, the poetry writing on the Piano at top of kitchin bin VERY TOP if you want it back.

and Oblige Viv.

Beetrooty colonels explain to the Lounge Bar how, in the 'Last Show',
they had a marvellous time, and how we need a new war

if we are going to get this Great Country back on its feet, sir
(also all beards should be shaved: also the Dole should be stopped).

Life still goes on and *It isn't the end of the world* (the child-soothing
platitudes weaken now Cruise proves them potentially false).

Lieder's no art against these sorry times (anguished Paramour likens
mountainy crags and a crow to the flint heart of his Frau).

Dear sir,

have done some hoover of the front room. but am going now be back tomorrow morning if you can oblige with next week money same as last time. Only my sister. not the one in Australia the other one here. was standing at the bus station when boys threw bottles and ones broken glass flew up and cut leg BAD CUT. only about ten also, she says so must go and help as she is lost a husband recently too. I tell you no one knows how bad it is here with these children ALL OVER. They will be the death of us no mistake. also the world sitution no better, America Russia jews and Arabians irish and such. what can you do as it gets worse like one of yr poetry Works that I saw when cleaning desk with wax which I need more of soon as possible please. The same as in the empty tin. but well what can you do only get on with it. as you cant' sort it all out can you? we are like the man in music Hall song that goes he play his ~~Uka uker~~ Youkalaylee while the ship went down. only we all have problems like my sister and Goverments so can only carry on best we can, the next weeks money this week please as am short due to various things and the new wax pollish
Viv.

PS. doctor said it is not SO bad but has had 6 stitch.

Glossy black slices of smooth slab are all laid facing towards due
East – in the twerpish conceit sunrise might pleasure them *now*!

Glittery gilt lists the names and the dates and the bullshit about
them
- 'Fell Asleep', 'Gone to Rest' (tcha!), 'Resting in Jesus' Arms' (pah!).

'Gone Where We'll All Join Again on the Happy Shore Everafter'
(spew, vomit, puke, throw-up, retch), 'Went Without Saying
Goodbye'.

Inside a shed with the Council's coat-of-arms blazoned on it
there is a Flymo and spades. Here comes a gent with a pick:

'Wouldn't it make you want to dip your bread in the piss-pot
– some of the bilge they write there? Fuckin daft sods' (he opines).

Sweet peas are cunningly wrought in a huge pink crucifix resting
fresh on damp just-replaced turf. Wet clay outlines a new slot.

Biro-smudged sympathy-cards blow about and one is signed 'Viv, The
Depest Regrett Always Felt' (it shows a wren on a wreath).

On a diminutive gravy-hued sandstone wafer is chiselled
that which, despite mawkishness, prompts a sharp intake of breath.

Aged 10.
Little Boy,
We Would Not
Wake You To
Suffer Again.

Oh sir,

only I havnt known. which way to TURN since the Funeral. It was the sisters youngest such a good lad too and only ten it seems wrong. somehow, and they would play in the streets though they was told often enough GOD only knows. So it was a bus when they was playing foot-ball and the poor little mite had gone when they got him. to the Hospitle so that is why I didnt' come for 3 days but was in the morning and hope you find this note behind the tea pot and with thanks for the new Polish which have done the desk and chairs with. My oldest Trevor has been TOWER OF strenth since tragdy but <u>will</u> get those tatoos just like his DAD in that way just last week got MAM done on his hand which is nice he is a good lad to his Mother and a Tower. So can I have last weeks moneys though I did not come and not have money next week instead. Only the flowers which was a cross of pink flowers. very nicely done. do cost such a lot not that you bigrudge it do you when its your own Sisters youngest? So if you could leave it buy the dusters and furnature wax it will befine tomorrow.

Obliged, Viv.

PS we take her to the zoo next weekend to take her out of herself. the sister. as it will be a nice change our Trevor says.

'Them animals is disgusting.'

In London Zoo is a large flat painted Disneyesque lion
sporting a circular hole cut where the face ought to be.

On its reverse is a step upon which the visitor stands and
puts his own face through the hole – so that he may be thus snapped.

So, the resultant photograph shows the face of a friend or
relative grinning like mad out of a leonine frame.

This seems to be a very popular piece of equipment –
Arabs in nightshirts and Japs queue with Jews. Polaroids click.

Tabloids blown underfoot headline a couple of global débâcles.
Gran, from the lion's mouth, leers: toothless, cadaverous, blithe.

Oh it is very funny to put your head through the facial
orifice of a joke lion – races and creeds are agreed.

Down the old Monkey House there is a *Cercopithecus* wanking
and a baboon (with its thumb stuck up its arse) to revile.

Dear Sir didnt come in yesterday as planned as I lost key and how it happened was this. that we went to zoo with sister and the children which was the sister lost her youngest. And while we was throwing a ten pence for luck onto back of Allergator corcodile which is in Tropical House it must have fell from my purse. Everyone throws money for luck onto back of this Reptille and his pool is FULL of two P ten P and 5P pieces which bring GOOD LUCK to thrower. So had to go yesterday to see if the keeper had found it. he had and said they empty pool every month and spend money. It buys keepers there beer he says they get POUNDS so I got key back that is why I am here today instead but unfortunatly have by ACCIDENT spoilt one of your papers with poetry on it that was on yr desk as I threw it on the Parkray by mistake. and hope this is no inconvenience or can you do another one instead? Sister much better since outing but oldest boy Trev in trouble with police who came last night to house but I dont believe it as he is a good boy. But she is perking up a bit now and was cheerful at weekend and my boy took a Poloid Photo of her with head through a LION which was V. funny and makes her laugh which is good for her. Police say he has mugged but it canot be as he is GOOD BOY.

faithly VIV. p.s. worse things happen at SEA!

'Life is too black as he paints it' and 'Reading's nastiness sometimes
seems a bit over the top' thinks a review – so does *he*.

Too black and over the top, though, is what the Actual often
happens to be, I'm afraid. He don't *invent* it, you know.

Take, for example, some snippets from last week's dailies before they're
screwed up to light the Parkray: Birmingham, March '83,

on her allotment in King's Heath, picking daffodils, Dr
Dorris McCutcheon (retired) pauses to look at her veg.

Dr McCutcheon (aged 81) does not know that behind her,
Dennis (aged 36) lurks, clutching an old iron bar.

Unemployed labourer Dennis Bowering sneaks up behind her,
bashes her over the head – jaw, nose and cheek are smashed-in.

Dennis then drags her until he has got her into the tool-shed,
strikes her again and again, there is a sexual assault,

also a watch and some money worth less than ten pounds are stolen.
'Is an appalling offence...' Bowering is told by the Judge.

Amateur frogmen discover a pair of human legs buried
Mafia-style in cement, deep in an Austrian lake.

Smugly, Americans rail over KA 007;
angrily, Moscow retorts. Hokkaido fishermen find

five human bits of meat, one faceless limbless female Caucasian,
shirts, empty briefcases, shoes, fragments of little child's coat,

pieces of movable section of wing of a 747,
one piece of human back flesh (in salmon-fishermen's nets),

one headless human too mangled to ascertain what the sex is.
USA/USSR butcher a Boeing like chess

(probably civil jumbos *are* used for Intelligence business;
pity the poor sods on board don't have the chance to opt out).

Sexual outrage on woman of 88 robbed of her savings.
Finger found stuck on barbed wire. Too black and over the top.

Clearly we no longer hold *H. sapiens* in great reverence
(which situation, alas, no elegiacs can fix).

What do they think they're playing at, then, these Poetry Wallahs?
Grub St. reviewing its own lame valedictory bunk.

NOTE: KA 007: in September 1983 a Soviet fighter plane shot down a South Korean airliner when all 269 passengers were killed, causing a brief stir.

dear Sir,

well I have hooverd and wax pollish the desk so I will collect money tomorrow. There is trouble on our block since my Tom plays the bones to tunes of George Formby and was due to give a TURN at the club tonight but was paralitic last night and WOULD try to practise and of course one of them. the bones. went over next door and the woman there that has the bitch that MARLD the child well her bitch grabs the bone but my Tom shouts abuse and. of course the outcome is there is a window broke. Which the man next door have only just mended after the last trouble. so we will see how it goes tonight at the Club he does that one he played his Youkerlaylie as the Ship Went down. and I know how He felt, because it is the same with my eldest Trevor who is REPRIMANDED IN CUSTARDY as the policeman put it who is a nice man but I know my lad is innerscent of that awful thing they say he done. But these things are sent to TRY Us as my Man says and I hope he plays his bones well tonight. just like he did that year we were in the T.V. show Mr and Mrs, did you know we were in it? yes in Llandudno and he entertained the crowds they were in stitches when the ONE MAN BAND never turned up. so I have used up all the Johnsons Wax again so please oblige, We all have problems even the different Parlerments, also the police Forces. as well as me, and you with Yr writings

Viv, P.S. we can only carry on the best we can manage

Down at the PDSA there's a queue of unprepossessing
buggered-up budgies and dogs. Someone is telling how Rex

quite unaccountably ('Never been known to act like it previous')
set on the nipper next door, and must now 'get put to sleep'.

'Even although he has done such a thing – and that to a kiddy –
I can't help loving him still – you *have* to stand by your own.'

'That's what I feels about my eldest (Trev) – they've done him
for mugging –
still, you *must* still love your own; if he's bad, he's *still* my boy.'

Cotton wool tenderly placed in a shoe-box comforts a frail life.
There is much love at the Vet's – even for bad dogs and Trev.

* * *

Was one time anchored in forty
fathom near unto the shore
of Mascarenhas Island.
Landed, we found blue pigeons
so tame as to suffer us
to capture them by our hands
so that we killed and roasted
above two hundred the first day.
Also we took many others –
grey paraquets, wild geese
and penguins (which last hath but stumps
for wings, so cannot fly).
Most entertaining to catch
a paraquet and make it
cry aloud till the rest
of its kind flocked round it and thus
enabled themselves to be caught.
Twenty five turtle, lying
under one tree, was taken.

On then to St Mary's Island,
where we careened, and thence
stood for the Straights of Sunda.

At 5° 30′
south of the line, the alarm
'Fire!' was raised – the steward
had gone below for brandy,
thrust candle into the hole
of a cask on the tier above
whence he drew his spirits, and when
removing his candle, a spark
had fell from the wick down the bung,
igniting the spirit. He poured
water unto the cask,
by which we had thought to choke it.

But the flames, reviving, blew out
the cask ends, when the fire
reached to a heap of coals
stowed there, which, lighted, gave off
a thick sulphureous smoke
thwarting attempts to extinguish it.

In this emergency
I appealed to the supercargo
to cast overboard all powder.
But (stubborn, arrogant, greedy,
as so many of his class)
he refused. Says he 'To throw
our powder away is to risk
attack from our enemies'.

Meantime the rage of the fire
augmented more and more.
We scuttled decks that greater
floods of water could be
got into ye hold, but all
attempts proved vain.

                                        I resolved
to summon the carpenters
with augers to bore the hull
that water might enter below
and quench the flames.

                                        But our oil
ignited then, d'ye see?,
and with sixty five good men
I stood on deck by the main
hatchway receiving buckets
when the powder, 300 kegs,
was reached.

The vessel blew up
into the air with one hundred
and nineteen souls: a moment
afterwards, not one single
human being was seen:
believing myself to be launched
into eternity,
I cried out aloud for Mercy.

Some slender remnant of life
and resolution still lurked
in my heart. I gained the wreck,
as was gone to a thousand pieces,
clung to a yard.

The long-boat,
got off afore the explosion
by a deserting faction,
now, in the very worst
of my extremity,
ran to the place with all speed,
whereat the trumpeter
threw out a line by which
I obtained that frail haven
of temporary ease,
and hymned being simply extant.

Cast up, one time, wrecked,
on bleak Patagonia
out of the Wager, Indiaman,
Commodore Anson's squadron.
Six years, afore we reached home.

Only food, shellfish and raw seal –
as we managed to stone unto death
or found dead, raw, rank, rotted.

Reduced thus to misery,
and so emaciated,
we scarce resembled mankind.
At nights in hail and snow
with naught but open beach
to lay down upon in order
to procure a little rest –
oftentimes having to pull off
the few rags I was left wearing,
it being impossible
to sleep with them on for the vermin
as by that time swarmed about them;
albeit, I often removed
my sark and, laying it down
on a boulder, beat it hard
with an huge stone, hoping to slay
an hundred of them at once,
for it were endless work
to pick them off one by one.
What we suffered from this
was worse even than the hunger.
But we were cleanly compared
of our captain, for I could compare
his body to nothing more like
an ant hill, so many thousand
of vermin crawling over it;
for he were past attempting
to rid himself in the least
of this torment, as he had quite
lost himself, not recollecting
our names that were about him,
nor his own. His beard as long

as an hermit's: that and his face
being besmirched of filth
from having been long accustomed
himself to sleep on a bag
in which he kept stinking seal meat
(which prudent measure he took
to prevent our getting at it
as he slept). His legs swelled huge
as mill-posts, whilst his torso
was as a skin packet of bones –
and upon bleached seal bones he played
hour after hour in uncanny
tattoo as to harmonise
with a wordless mindless dirge
as he moithered, moithered, moithered,
weird, xysterical airs,
yea, even unto the end.

Was one time cast on Oroolong,
when the Antelope packet went down.
The king of Cooroora
succoured us, gave us meat,
in return of which we shewed him
the swivel as we had salvaged
out of the wreck, and the six-
pounder and our small-arms.
He and his natives were thrilled
and astonished. A flying squirrel
having settled upon a tree
nearby, our captain's servant
loaded his musquet, shot it.
Seeing the animal drop
off of a lofty tree's top,
without, apparently,
anything passing to it,
they ran to take it up;
when, perceiving the holes,
they chuckled, evidenced glee
and begged to be allowed
guns for themselves that they might
do slaughter of their near neighbours
whom they were desirous to see
fall, full of holes, as this,
dead in great quantity.
We acquiesced.

They made
great execution with these,
our fire-arms, puzzling their foes,
who could not comprehend
how that their people dropped
without receiving any
apparent blow. Though holes
were seen in their bodies, they couldn't
divine by what agency
they were thus, in a moment, deprived
of motion and life. The whole
of the prisoners taken was shot.

We objected upon this last,
explained inhumanity
unto ye simple minds.

Their king gave unto us then
a kind of victory banquet,
whereat one tar of our number,
who out of the wreck had saved
an Italian violin
and had the bowing of it,
struck up. I know not whether
twas due to the victory,
or the feast, or to the grog
of which we allowed them a plenty,
or whether the fiddle musick;
but, be it whichever, they reeled,
cavorted like monkeys and fell
euphoric with our company
unto ye general dust.

Sailed one time aboard
trawler the Lucky Dragon,
crew o' 23,
hundred miles off Bikini,
in the March of '54.

Tars was all below
down in the a'ter-cabin;
crew man, Suzuki,
run abaft a-hollering
'The sun rises in the West!'

Hands mustered on deck,
saw, to larboard, a fireball,
like a rainbow brand,
rise up from ye horizon,
silent, that was the queer thing.

Minutes passed; the blast
suddenly shook the ocean,
shuddered our whole hulk,
hands was belayed with affright,
none, howsomdever, hurt (*then*).

But the skies turned *strange* –
misty wi' weird white ashes
as *swirled*, d'ye see?,
down onto decks, men, rigging...
That ash made us ill (*later*).

Most awful, terrific form
shipwreck can take is fire;
where the unfortunate
victims has only two
alternatives – to seek death
in one element in order
to avoid it in another.

One time the enemy's powder
(with whom we was close-engaged)
took fire – match left a-purpose
by their skipper, damn his eyes –
both the vessels blew up,
most violent dreadful explosion.

We, the spectators, ourselves
were the poor players also
in the bloody scene – some thinking
maybe it were the Last Judgement,
confounded, unable to gauge
whether or no we beheld it –
two ships hurled up on high
two hundred fathoms in air,
where there was formed a mountain
of fire, water and wreck;
dread conflagration below,
cannon unpeeling above,
rending of masts and planks,
ripping of canvas and cordage,
screams, like stuck pigs, of brent tars.

When the ship first took fire
I was blowed clean from the forecastle,
fell back into the sea
where I remained under water
unable to gain ye surface,
struggled as one afeared
of drowning, got up and seized
a bulk of mast as I found
nearby.

Saw floating about
divers wounded and dead –
two half bodies, with still
some remnant of life, a-rising
and sinking, rising and sinking,
leaving the deep dyed pink.
Deplorable to behold
scores of limbs and fragments
of bodies – most of them spitted
on splintered timbers and spars.

Survivors we boarded a boat
almost entire from the wreck.
Most of us vomited constant
from swallowing pints of sea water.

I suffered long and swelled
to a surprising degree,
all my hair, face and one side
of my body were brent with powder;
bled at the mouth, nose, ears
(I know not whether this
be the effect of powder,
by swelling up the vessels
containing the blood of our bodies
to such extent that the ends
of the veins open and ooze it;
or whether it be occasioned
by the great noise and violent
motion in the same organs –
but let it happen which way
it will, there was no room there then
for consulting of physicians).

Thro the long night some sang,
attempting to keep up spirits.
Merciful Providence
preserving some measure of wine
and rum from the hold, the mate
contrived then to engineer
a musical instrument
on which he made bold to play.

Since I have so often felt
the malignant influence
of the stars presiding over
the seas, and by adverse fortune
lost all the wealth which, with such
trouble and care, I amassed,
it has been no source of pleasure
recalling to memory
the disasters that have assailed us.

Still, as a singer a song
or an old player an air,
I am impelled to convey
salt observations, a tar's
chantey habit, d'ye see?

I know not whether we've bid
adieu to the sea, or whether
we shall set forth again
where we have known such mischief;
whether traverse the ocean
in quest of a little wealth;
or rest in quiet and consume
what our relations have left us.

Our strange propensity
to undertake voyages,
alike to that of gaming –
whatever adversity
befalls us, we trust, at length,
prosperity shall o'ertake us,
therefore continue to play.

So with us at sea,
for, whatever calamity
we meet with, we hope for some
chance opportunity
to indemnify our losses.

And shall it, now, be counted
as ye dignified defiance
in us towards our fateful
merciless element,
or gull naiveté,
cousin to recklessness,
that, e'en in pitching Gulphward,
our salt kind brings forth chanteys?

* * *

Who would have thought it Sir, actually putting ME in a WRITING!
me and the Capting and ALL. What a turn up for the books.

Only, I must say I do not know HOW them people in poems
manage to say what they want – you know, in funny short lines,

or like what YOU do with them ones of yours sir, made of two lines like.
Still, when you're USED to it like, then you can speak natural.

Only, the newspaper man said that you was TRYING to sound like
low classes voices and that, only you wasn't no good –

you know, the CUTTING you left on yr desk top when I was waxing –
you know, that CRICKET which said you wasn't no good at all?

when you got TERRIBLE, stamping and raging calling him stupid
and how the man was a FOOL, which was the day you took DRINK.

'What is to one class of minds and perceptions exaggeration,
is to another plain truth' (Dickens remarks in a brief

preface to *Chuzzlewit*). 'I have not touched one character straight from
life, but some counterpart of that very character has

asked me, incredulous, "Really now *did you* ever see, *really*,
anyone *really* like that?"' (this is the gist, not precise).

Well I can tell that old cricket that this is JUST how we speaks like,
me and the Capting and all (only not just in two lines).

One time, returning to home port, fell in with Englishman (16-gunner) bound England from Spain; hailed her heave-to and belay.

After a skirmish we forced her to strike her colours and seized her. Auctioned her off at Rochelle; carried the prize to Bordeaux.

Our tars had been so long absent from home that now we indulged in every extravagant vice, ere we be called to ye Deep.

Merchants advanced us, without hesitation, money and goods on promise of that which was our share of the booty, d'ye see?

We spent the night in whatever amusements best pleased our fancy – claret and gore and the stench of ye rank pox-festered trulls.

We spent the next day traversing the town in masquerade, ranting, had ourselves carried in chairs, lighted with torches, at noon.

As we caroused thus abroad we caused music, plucked forth from gambas
boldly, t'embellish the raw, rude Dionysian debauch.

And the drear consequence of this gross wanton mass indiscretion was the untimely demise of damned near all the whole crew.

Jimmy 'The Beard' Ferrozzo, aged 40, Manager of the
Condor Club, where I now work (down San Francisco's North Beach),

died when the stage-prop piano we use for Carol the stripper pinned him tight into the roof, causing his breathing to stop.

Mr Boyd Stephens, the medical guy who did the autopsy,
said that Ferrozzo was pressed so tight he couldn't inhale,

said that 'Compression Asphyxia' is the name of the ball-game – pressure had squashed up the chest so hard it couldn't expand.

I have been Caretaker down at the topless Condor Club now for, must be a couple of years. When I unlocked, 9 a.m.,

I found Ferrozzo draped over his girlfriend (23-year-old
Trixie – this slag from the Club, nude Go-Go dancer, you know?).

She had no clothes on and she was stuck, screaming, under him – it was
three hours before she could be freed by the cops from the raised

Steinway, a prop they have used at the Club for 2 decades almost
(topless star Carol descends, sprawled on the keys, to the stage).

Even now, no one knows what caused the joke piano to rise up
into the ceiling, 12 ft., pinning Ferrozzo and Trix.

Police say the motor that operates on the lifting device had
burned out and couldn't be switched so as to bring it back down.

Some way the Manager's body had kept her 2 or 3 inches
off of the ceiling and stopped Trixie herself being crushed.

Det. Whitney Gunther says: 'She was so drunk she doesn't remember
laying down nude on the strings inside the grand – she just knows

sometime that a.m. she woke up to hear the twanging of taut wires.'
Man! What an Exit, you know? Welter of plucked gut and spunk.

Only, because it has broke (I.T.V.) we HAD to watch 'Seasars' –
stories about the roam Kings, dirty disgusting old lot.

One of them dressed up in smelly old skins and rushed out at captives
wounding there PRIVATES with KNIFE. also had LOVED his own Mam.

this is called 'Narrow' which plays on a fiddle, all the time Roam burnd
but why it Brakes is because. my man has FIXED it last week

Also my mack is at cleaners because of kiddies which MARK it
ever so bad with their spit. They should be children of Roam –

what with the way they go on with their dirty, horrible, habbits
One of which made them all HEAR while he plays music all nite.

This one is known as 'Callegulum' which is v. funny name for
King but is THERE on t.v. So must be right. it is pink

leather effect with a belt and the reason why there is broken glass on Barometer is: cutting a LONG story short.

My man is playing it just as a banjo, being the SAME SHAPE, singing the George Formby Song. and he has drop it on FLOOR

SO that the glass and the silvery stuff you get in it all come out and can not be got back. One of them SAWED men in half

also he has a poor soul stabbed to death with terrible pen nibs also a mans' brains flogged out using a CHAIN for three days

which is the same sort of thing that you get in newspaper these days. what with the Irish and that. so I have bought a new GAMP.

That is because of the Mack but he also made FATHER's go to SEE their own kiddies killed dead, that was the worst thing of all

so it has broke and the needle now ALWAYS points to the STORMY – he is a fool to have PLAYED (Formby) But ROAM is BAD TIME

Nero springs out girt in lynx pelts and slits slave's dick with a razor... *ROAM is BAD TIME*, as is Wolves: January '84,

19-year-olds Brian Johnson and friend Troy Blakeway are jogging, that they may catch the last bus, after a disco in town.

Leaving the Old Vic Hotel, Wolverhampton, they are pursued by 25 rampaging youths (West Indians, it appears).

Johnson leaps onto a bus but is stabbed twice just as the doors close (two deep long cuts in the thigh, 15 and 12 inches long).

At the Royal Hospital he receives more than seventy stitches. Blakeway is knifed in the back, trying to flee from the mob –

in the deep 6-inch-long gash he gets thirty stitches; a sobbing middle-aged parent attends (whose hand a nurse gently pats).

'Very sharp instruments must have been used for making these nasty injuries' C.I.D. says (Johnson and Blakeway concur).

It has not been without usefulness that the Press has administered
wholesale mad slovenly filth, glibly in apposite prose,

for it has wholly anaesthetised us to what we would either
break under horror of, or, join in, encouraged by trends.

Horrible headlines don't penetrate. Pongoid crania carry
on as though nothing were wrong. *Homo autophagous*, Inc.

Gillian Weaver aged 22 walking 4-year-old daughter
home when a girl and three men – hang on, this isn't just *news*:

Gillian Weaver aged 22 walking 4-year-old daughter
home when a girl and three men push her to pavement and steal

£3 from purse – she sits weeping and nursing 4-year-old (let's not
wax sentimental re kids; let's stick to facts, here *are* facts).

As she sits weeping and hugging her daughter, one of the muggers
comes back and razors her thus **slashes her face 50 times**

(this is the Mirror and not *myself* – I have no axe to grind, right?)
C.I.D. seeks three blacks plus one spotty, ginger-haired white.

Meanwhile, I've gotten the 5-Minute Uke Course (Guaranteed
Foolproof) –
plinkplinka plinkplinka plonk plinkplinka plinkplinka plonk.

Grans are bewildered by post-Coronation disintegration;
offspring of offspring of *their* offspring infest and despoil.

This is the Age Of The Greatly Bewildered Granny & Grandad,
shitlessly scared by the bad, mindless and jobless and young;

also the Age Of The Dispossessed Young, with nothing to lose by
horribly hurting their sires, babies and cripples, and whose

governments, freely elected and otherwise, function by mores
not altogether removed from their own bestial codes –

those sort of policies, that sort of hardware do not imply much
kindly respect for *H. sap*, mindless and jobless and young...

Maybe we're better off under the Civic Centre than up there
what with the LUTEing and that – them inner-cities is BAD,

maybe we're better off here in his WRITINGS, orrible though they
often is sometimes, than THERE – out in that awful real-life

what with its madness and sometimes I thinks the Capting's the only
sane one among the whole lot – Four or five leagues West-sou'west!

Steadily bear away under a reefed lug foresail, ye bilge rats,
synne rises firey and red – sure indycation o' gales,

we have entrapped us a sea-mew and served the blood to ye weakest
members of crew, and myself? Liver and heart and ye guts.

For accompanying singing, the haunting harmony of the Uke has no superior! Soft summer nights and the Uke are inseparable pals! To wintery jollities the Uke adds zip and sparkle! Too much mystery and confusion have shrouded Uke playing! The Uke is an instrument for the best accompanying of happytime songs! Beautiful and very unusual effects can be achieved! You can learn to play richly harmonious accompaniments *in only a few minutes* by this New Method, and when you have done that **you have accomplished a great deal!**

'This is not Poetry, this is reality, untreated, nasty',
'This is demotic and cheap', 'This is mere caricature',

'This is just relishing violent, nasty...' so on and so forth,
Grub St. reviewing its own lame valedictory tosh –

Don't you go brooding and brooding and getting all of a state sir
just cos the LITARY GENT don't seem to like your nice books.

Like the old man used to always say When we wants YOU to chirp-up,
matey, we'll rattle the cage' – don't heed their old tommy-rot.

Grasp the pick lightly between thumb and first finger of right hand. Do not pinch! Move tip of pick back and forth across all four strings. Let that wrist hang loose! Start slow and then increase speed until you produce a smooth, even tone. Well done! The speed you move the pick across the strings will depend on what we call *tempo* (that means *time*) of the number you're accompanying! Well done! **That sounds just dandy**!

These are the questions that Councillors mean to raise at the
Meeting:
how much promethium remains? Has there been tritium used?

Why did the Army deny there was any contamination?
How do they mean to assure residents no risk remains?

What was the level of contamination? Where had it come from?
What is a 'low level' leak? Why was the public not told?

Why has the Army consistently issued flagrant denials
that any toxin remained after these secret 'events'?

Now you are ready for those oldies we know and love! Yes *Sir*! Sing, hum, or whistle the tune as you play! Play each chord as indicated until a new chord is shown. Do not change until you see another chord indicated! Everyone's just got to join in and **sing right along there**!

Carrying on as though things were O.K. is what we are good at –
fall-out-proof bunkers are built, orbiting space stations planned.

Only, it's worse in the papers than what you stick in your writings, what with I seen a man knocked down WITH MY OWN EYES by black man and poor soul that was muged was ON CRUTCHES and that is gospel truth but not as bad as burning baby with CIG END which some swine done to get purse from mother of two. So even if they are out of work it is NOT RIGHT they should hurt their own townpeoples. Any road it is too late now so we can just HOPE FOR BEST which I DO, and will only live in shelter or outer spaces if there is no other possible. But will NOT eat sardines morning noon and night.

Finally now we return to the deep, and reaching our dim craft
drag her black hull through safe shale down to the fathomless
brine.

Next, to the dark-bellied vessel we carry white sails and main-mast,
lifting aboard her the sheep, white tup and black ewe, and now,

heavily laden with misery, shedding tears in abundance,
hark to our skipper's command, nimble in wit and resource.

Thus we embark while astern of us rise up sail-swelling breezes
surging the blue-prowed ship forth, 12 knots with main-skysail set.

So, d'ye see, after putting our gear and tackle in order,
all we can do is observe, course set by helmsman and wind.

Thus with full canvas we traverse the waters into ye blackness;
tenebrose, fog-bound, the bar, into the tow of the stream.

Here is perpetual smoke of a city unpierced by sunlight
where ye Cimmerians dwell, unvisible from above.

Here we make fast and drive up from the bilges, bleating, the
stunned sheep
into these bunkers of lead, granite and greyness and stench.

Wend your luff, messmates, and let go the skysail halliards, mister,
cut the brace pennants and stays, reef the fore-topgallant in,

falling barometer, send down the skysail yard from aloft, sir,
strum with felt pick back and forth, lightly across all four strings,

all sail should be double-gasketted, stow the mainsail and cross-jack,
make yr pentameters taut: two-and-a-half feet times two,

bend ye now three lower storm-staysails and a storm spanker, mister,
take in the three upper tops, close-reef the foresail, F sharp,

tighten the B string and place finger at the back of the second
fret of the A string and keep spondees and dactyls close-clewed,

trim yr heroic hexameter (or it may be dactylic),
splice the pentameter aft, finger yr frets as ye go

surely we shouldn't be speaking like this sir, not in Allergic
Dis Talk, taint natural-like: I'm goin back to me prawse

only I've not been old self since they started the TREATMENT but do not WORRY as they SWEAR it is non malingerent tumer ONLY which only in my opinion only needs GOOD TONIC and will soon be old self again but sometimes feeling bit on queer side that is to be expected the doctor say, but what with one thing and another and the worry over eldest boy in trouble with LAW I do not know which way to turn but I do wonder when you read these cases what do the mothers think. and the father's. because they are all some mothers children which loves them I should say. Even if they are vilent crimnal. So will soon be back on feet again but this worry is worrying with internashnal TROUBLE brewing as the BULLETIN says and I do not feel so perky as previous. So will sign of for the present

if I could only be just this once pardoned Spawndies and Doctale
which we has never heard of down at the Ten-Storey-Flats.

The Triple Roll is one of the prettiest of all Uke strokes! It is a very simple stroke too, when analyzed! Just follow the simple stages below one step at a time! Soon you will get the 'knack'! Yes *Sir*!

Bring forefinger down across all four strings where neck joins body of Uke. Bring that old fingernail down so that it glides smoothly on the strings. That sounds just swell! Practise this again and again and again! **Then follow with thumb down**. After forefinger leaves last string bring ball of thumb down across strings. **Then bring first finger up**. As thumb leaves last string, bring the ball or fleshy part of forefinger up across all four strings. Yes *Sir*! Forefinger should begin to go up the very second that little old thumb leaves the last string! Say! That sounds like a million dollars! You, good buddy, have just mastered yourself the **TRIPLE ROLL!!!**

I had believed myself fairly inured to foolishness after
6 months for Reuter's in parched mad bloody Lebanon, but

leaving the hotel that morning (with Dickie Pratt, of the Mirror),
in the main street of Sidon, I was presented with this:

out from the shade of the shelled former Admin. Offices stepped a
miniature, wielding a huge glinting black muzzle and stock,

just as a fat juicy jeep of Israelis swung into vision.
Three or four seconds he stood, sputtering hail at the jeep –

windscreen-glass frosted and one of the front seat occupants oozed
red,
there was a crackle of fire, ten or so seconds, and then,

as from a colander, into the pavement streamed out the juices
of the assailant, a slight soldier/homunculus. Well,

nobody looks for a *motive* from these Old Testament shitters –
thick hate is still in the genes. I learned the boy was aged 12.

Say! At the outset, the beginner may find his fingers just a little bit stiff and clumsy but this disappears quickly after a little practice! So why not keep right on along gut-pluck-a-plickin come rain or come shine! Yes *Sir*! Let's start with the little finger down where the neck joins the body...

'Tries to be shocking', 'Predictable, coarse, insensitive, tasteless...'
when I want you to chirp-up, matey, I'll rattle the cage.

Say! What you need to do each day is keep that little old Uke in tune! Yes *Sir*! Who wants to hear an out-of-tune Uke? That's right! – Nobody! Say! Why not tune that Uke right now? O.K. let's go! You need a piano to help you. Tune A string to A on piano. Tune D string to sound the same as D on piano. Tune F-Sharp string and B string to sound like those notes on piano. Get it? If you do not know where these notes are located on piano then ask some guy who's a pianist to show you. Right?

What with the waiting and not knowing what on earth is the matter
up in the cities and that. Still, it was awful up there

what with last Wednesday that one what married him from the Top Flats
pushing the babby she was, down by the Preesint new shops,

suddenly found erself total surrounded by what-do-you-call-em?
them Rasterfastium blacks; you know, the ones with the LOCKS.

One got er purse but the pleece come and then the LEADER a FAT man
snatched up the babby and STABBED – right in the EYE with a pen,

animals that's what I think of them monsters horrible wild BEASTS
not safe to walk in the streets – not that we could NOW, of course

only it's funny for us being down here under the Civict
Centre – I thought it was all Underground Car Parks and that.

During this voyage ye heavens has been so dree overcast that
no observation by stars, nor yet by sun can be got.

Little round light like a tremulous faint star streams along sparking,
blazes blue, shoots shroud to shroud, running along ye main yard,

stays half the night with us, settles on fore-shrouds. Spaniards call it
Fire of St Elmo – be damned! Fire of ye Devil, it be.

Only the Capting gets mixed up about his time in the Navy –
muddles it up with them YARNS. You know, them ones what you READ,

not as I'm one for the books and that what with doing the housewort
(no Womans Libbance for ME, what with that much things to do.

get on with THIS Viv and THAT Viv and, well you has to LIVE
don't you?
that's what I think, any road). Close-clew your sails, mates, avast,

shew a reefed foresail to steer by and run for harbour my buckoes,
oakum discharged from hull's seams; pipe up all hands to the pumps!

Make ye now ready for Davy Jones, messmates, get ye the strings tuned,
highest grade sheep's gut, they be – list to the boatman, belay,

as o'er the stream we glide borne by the rolling tide chanting and rowing…
Place your 3rd finger behind 3rd fret of 4th string and strum

Only I've never been happy but what I'm pottering, I ain't –
always the pottering sort, that's why I hates coming DOWN

mind you the Powertree Bloke and the Capting doesn't arf GABBLE –
what with the Capting his YARNS: tother keeps chaingin is VOICE

anyone'd think they was Everyone All Times Everywhere, way they
gabbles and rambles and that: still, they can't help it, poor souls.

Whatsisname says to me 'Viv you're the life and soul of the party' –
Viv, he says, MEANS life, you know (in Greek or Lating or French)

plīnkplĭnkă | plīnkplĭnkă | plīnkplĭnkă | plīnkplīnk | plīnkplĭnkă | plīnkplīnk
plīnkplĭnkă | plīnkplĭnkă | plōnk || plīnkplĭnkă | plīnkplĭnkă | plōnk

GOING ON

(1985)

[Bit of a habit, this feigned indignation,
various forms, Elegiacs, Alcmanics...
gets like a game, the old global débâcles.
Just Going On remains possible through the
slick prestidigital art of Not Caring/Hopelessly Caring.]

Muse! Sing the Rasta. who stabbed out a
baby's eye with a Biro
   thereby persuading its mum
   that she should give him her purse

   [Halve the hexameter after three
   dactyls, making it 2 lines;
      halve the pentameter thus –
      this way it fits on the page.]

down in the crazed uriniferous
subway underneath Blake St
   (leading to Wordsworth Estate)
   spattered with drooled viscid spawl.

   [Squirrelprick Press is producing my
   latest, *Blood Drops in Distich*,
      hand-deckled limp-covered rag,
      Special Edition of ten.]

'Swear by Almighty...the evidence
I shall... and nothing but the...'
   'Sergeant Gillespie, please tell,
   in your own words, to the Court...'

'Constable Renton walked into the
charge room just a few moments
   after the time when Carliell
   had been allegedly punched

and he said "I'm sorry, Sarge, but I
caught him one with my ring like.
   Couldn't we sort something out?"
   I said "Get out of the room."

I said "I'm not putting my wife and
kids on the line for you, Renton."
  Carliell had been brought in drunk.'
  'Ladies and gentlemen of...

I submit that Mr Carliell was
struck a blow of such vicious...
  Call Mr Peter Lee...Now,
  you, on the night of... next cell...

tell the Court, please Mr Lee, what you
heard that night in the next cell.'
  'I could hear screaming, and he
  shouted "You've knocked out my eye.

Why have you done this?" he shouted, and
I could hear him like screaming...'
  'Constable Renton is charged,
  ladies and gentlemen of...'

I am traduced in the press (for a
poem weary of war-rent
  mad bloody Lebanon) as
  Antisemitic, Bad Hat.

No, no, not antisemitic, dears,
antibutchery only;
  both sides still deadlocked in hate,
  sanguin'ry as the O.T.

Literal Readers, Perverse Exe-
gesists bay for my spilt blood...
  Wait till the lit. mags. unleash
  my controversial next op. –

Muse!, sing the family *Strigidae*
hooting 'hooey' and 'hooey'
  down in a dell in the dark.
  Hooey and hooey and tosh.

['...you will not know me but...something in
common...both up at Oxford...
six years your junior – yet
both of us Balliol men!...']

All of you goat-esses be not so
Frisky, lest the bold he-goat
Rouseth himself to ye all!
Muses, begin the sweet song.

['...so my dear Lockhart I venture to
send these "Lyrical Fragments
Done Into English" in case
"Quarterly" readers may care...']

If 'tis your fancy to fasten your
Cloak-end on your right shoulder,
And you can stand an attack,
Get thee to Egypt forthwith.

We all grow grey at the temples and
Time's snow creeps down our cheek-bones;
We should be active while sap
Courses yet fresh in our joints.

['...Sir, I remain Yr. Obedient
Servant, Reverend Wolly,
Parsonage, May '35,
Claresmould-cum-Cowperly, Snotts.']

Eunica mocked me when I would have
Kissed her; then did she spit thrice
Into her bosom and said
'Neatherd, thy stench is obscene'.

Deborah Fallon, aged 19, is
handcuffed hugging an oak tree,
    forced by Rats Chapter to watch
    boyfriend (D. Cox, 22)

stabbed to death frenziedly, during which
she screams, pleads for her own life,
    but she is told she must die
    (strangled to death with a scarf).

This is because the Rats Chapter from
London ordered the killing
    (part of a scheme to 'sort out'
    Lucifer's Outlaws – a new

Northampton Chapter of Angels who
have been grassing about the
    whereabouts of an arms cache).
    Fallon and Cox are bumped off.

Serjeant-at-Arms (Stephen Parkinson)
and the President (Michael
    Bardell) of Lucifer's lot
    have been instructed to 'waste'

Fallon and Cox and, to indicate
that the Chapter has done it,
    they must slice one of her tits
    off and unpeel her scant pants...

[Which elegiacs aren't merely for
silly miscreant Angels,
    but all *H. sap* gone berserk –
    finished pernicious mad shits.]

'I am delighted to see that the
front page carries a photo
  of Douglas Fairbanks, the *dear*;
  I must have seen all his films,

younger and happier days, my boy,
younger, happier times when –'
  'No no no, Granny dear, no,
  this is no movie, but *real*:

"Prisoner threatens to murder a
hostage", this is the caption,
  "during the riot last week,
  Sexto gaol, Lima, Peru – " '

'Such a fine actor, dear boy, but I
can not think from which picture
  they can have taken that snap.
  Is it a pirate rôle, dear?'

'Gran, dearest Gran, this is *not* Douglas
Fairbanks cast as a pirate
  (or cast as anything else);
  this is a *prisoner*, see?

Listen, I'll read you the –' 'Oh such a
dashing figure he was though,
  I saw them all, you know, all,
  what I liked best was the one –'

' "Prisoners threatened to kill all the
hostaged lawyers, officials
  and other prisoners, if
  they were not given a safe

conduct and transport from gaol, and a
29-year-old woman
  (un-named) had first degree burns
  after the prisoners poured

petrol all over her, set her on
fire and watched as she –" ' 'Dear boy,
  I have remembered, of course,
  silly of me to forget!

This must be out of his picture of
'26, *The Black Pirate*.
   Oh, such a wonderful film,
   such a young thing I was, then.'

' "One of the hostages died after
being shot in the stomach –" '
   'He was a ladies' man, dear,
   oh such a ladies' man, yes.'

' "One of the victims was injured when
Sexto prisoners tried to
   cut off his legs with a saw –" '
   'Or could it be *Robin Hood*?

What was the date of dear *Robin Hood*,
darling? Dashing, so dashing.'
   ' "Statements from some of the guards
   say that an inmate cut out

one female hostage's tongue (she was
Carmen Montes, a typist)
   after she answered by phone
   questions put her by the press –" '

'No dear, I do not think somehow that
Mr Fairbanks was ever
   featured in *Carmen* at all.
   You are mistaken, dear boy.'

' "One of the victims, who worked at the
prison, Mr Rodolfo
   Farfan, was shot at point blank
   range in the abdomen and

slumped on his knees on a balcony
right in front of police and
   pressmen when inmates' demands
   (they wanted getaway vans)

met with refusal and –" ' 'Certainly,
dear, it is *The Black Pirate*,
   such a swashbuckling romp.
   More devilled kidneys, dear boy?'

Granny had been in the hospital
ever since she went funny.
   She was OK in herself –
   they made her do little things.

Each week some Volunteer Ladies came
(just to help with the Occu-
   pational Therapy) and
   very nice ladies they were.

This week the Volunteer Ladies were
making Grandmother bake scones;
   then, with a nice cup of tea,
   they let her gum one, still warm,

golden-brown luxury, scrumptiously
melting thickly-spread butter.
   Oh, she had always loved scones.
   This was her best treat for years.

Coroner Crawford-Clarke said that her
food had lodged in her larynx.
   'This would bring on very quick
   sudden death.' I ate the rest.

In City Centre it were [you will
notice Regional Accent
   tweely denoted by quaint
   phrasing] me sister were there

visiting like, an er lad as is
nearly seven were took short –
   needed to go to the bog.
   Well, Public Toilets was near,

so er just took im along to em
but they couldn't use *Ladies*
   (where er could look arter im)
   cos there were queue like outside.

So er sends im in nex door like to
Gents as seemed to be empty.
  Well, e seemed gorn a long time;
  so, when some feller comes by,

er says Just take a look in please an
see if nipper's OK like.
  So this bloke goes in you know.
  Sudden-like, out runs three youths

– what they ad done were to stuff the kid's
mouth with bog-paper roll then
  cut with a penknife is poor
  little dick orf and is balls.

Justice was seen to be done in South
Africa yesterday, thanks to
  laudable Judge Irving Steyn
  sitting in Rand Supreme Court.

Mr Francisco Quintino, a
56-year-old white man,
  shot dead a very bad rogue
  (called Macks Lerutia, a black)

whom he saw stealing the milk money
(63 cents) from a doorstep
  in the suburban all-white
  neighbourhood where he resides.

Judge Irving Steyn cleared Francisco of
all the charges against him.
  Also, sagacious Judge Steyn
  said how Francisco 'deserved

some sort of medal for what he had
done' and praised him for having
  selflessly acted – he said
  this was a real 'Civic Deed'.

Also, His Honour applauded the
'public service' which this Fran-
   cisco Quintino had done –
   curbed the unfortunate rash,

recently noted, of Milk Money
Thefts from decent white suburbs.
   (63 cents is about
   35 pence, English cash.)

Sadist Girl Guide Susan Hardwick and
boyfriend, 22-year-old
   Walsall man Martin Downes, robbed
   Mabel France (75).

Hardwick befriended the 'trusting old
fireman's widow' by running
   errands and doing odd jobs.
   Later, she 'relished' how Downes

put Mabel France through a 'wicked, per-
sistent, year's degradation'.
   Downes told the police he was 'skint',
   Mabel was 'just a good con'.

Those in the court heard accounts of how
Downes had burned the old lady
   using his cigarette-end,
   then had rubbed salt in the wounds.

Sometimes he fastened her eyes closed with
clothes-pegs, making her sit still*
   hour after hour after hour,
   whimpering, frightened and hurt.

* Often, it was alleged, with a plastic carnation stuck up her nose.

One day he tortured, then set loose, a
rat, which bit her; another
  (this was perhaps his most famed
  highly original trick),

he took a toilet brush, whipped up the
widow's skirts and performed – well,
  what, rather coyly, the court
  called an 'indecent assault'.

Often he forced her to swallow huge
doses of laxative tablets;
  she shat incontinently
  (Hardwick thought this was dead great).

Sometimes he plagued the old woman with
'phantom' voices he claimed were
  those of her husband and son
  (both of whom had been long dead).

£600 and her wedding ring
had been stolen and squandered.
  Mabel was too scared to tell
  police of the year-long ordeal.

Poor Martin wept uncontrollably
as his sentence was read out
  (4 years they gave him, and Sue
  got 6 months youth custody).

[...page after page of trite news reports
rehashed, vomiting squalor.
  Over-exposure to vile
  madness (from verse or the box)

makes for immunity. None of the
ghastly nasties he re-spews
  eases or mends with the mere
  telling *again* of its filth.]

Sí señor, sure we har claiming the
bomb as Glorious Blow by
  Forces of Liberate Dark
  Dictate Oppression. Too long

far have we, fathers and hrandfathers
forced to Slavery lifes hwich
  Army of Liberate fight
  struggles till all mens are dead!

Down with the generalísimo!
(not the present or last hwon,
  only the hwon pefore last),
  Viva la Muerte! señor,

Viva el excelentísimo
Señor conde de Torre-
  gamberro! Yes sirs my friend,
  what is the matter that some

dies for the Cause of the hwons that is
thinking right in this matters?
  This she's Political's War.
  Sure what are some person lifes?

We not Guerrillas amigo but
Counter-Anti-Guerrilla
  them was our Leaders but now –
  those is our Enemy, sí,

ow you say por favor now they has
showed False Ideologics.
  Terrorist Actions too bad;
  this why we take such Campaigns!

This very Positive Actions she
may have kill some who have no
doings with Rebels but so?
Bombs she not go off for fun.

Don't say amigo you not with the
understandings of why we
fights in montañas of South?
This are the struggles to death!

OK so 20 am dead and some
shrapnels goes to some peoples –
we har of People's own blood!
This is of why we shall fight!

Last bomb was not our bomb *that* was bomb
blown hwen Traitor who carries
gets it hexplosure too soon
killing himself and some mans.

Somehow you get mix up, señor, you
see we Neutral in all thing
this hwy the reasons hwe fights!
Freedoms to Govermans Farce!

Same Costa Rica but also with
Nicaraguan Border!
Now you mus hunderstand well
which why this bombs must hexplode.

Just hypothermia (Coroner
for St Pancras announces)
caused this particular death.
5-year-old Elliot Hinds'

mum and her boyfriend were said to have
got the idea from watching
some late-night film on T.V.
Anyway, Elliot died.

What he had done was to wet the bed
(that most heinous of child crimes)
 so, his mum's boyfriend took charge –
 held the boy under a shower

(full on the 'Cold' setting) for about
15 minutes. It seems that
 'Elliot usually screamed
 while being given cold showers'.

Sagely, the Coroner's jury re-
turns the old 'Misadventure'.
 'Ankle, I have little doubt,
 not through vindictiveness, but

probably just out of some way of
trying to discipline this lad,
 latched on to this form of cure.'
 (¼ hour's icy-cold shower.)

So, the Director of Public
Prosecutions decides that
 there is *not* gross negligence;
 therefore no Manslaughter charge.

Burning, per contra, is equally
efficacious in these things –
 30-year-old Terence Rose
 stoutly denied G.B.H.

Julie, his wife, though, explained how he
held their 2-year-old daughter
 '2 inches from the gas fire.
 It was full on' she alleged.

'Tara was screaming and tried to pro-
tect her legs with her hands, but
 he took no notice of her.
 Screaming and squirming she was.'

Some minutes later she 'messed on the
floor' and Terence informed her
    she was a 'dirty young bitch'.
    Mrs Rose told how he then

went for the slipper and hit the burnt
bottom and, as he smacked her
    'her flesh flew up in the air'
    (blistered, from burning, you see).

One night, about six weeks afterwards,
Terence went to the girl's room.
    Tara had peed in the bed.
    Terence was very annoyed.

Mrs Rose told how he 'called her a
dirty cow and I heard him
    dragging her into the loo.
    I heard him 26 times –

I heard him smacking her 26
times with the slipper. Her bottom'
    (still burnt) 'was bleeding' she said.
    Scars are still visible now.

[Clearly, then, some of us entertain
scant regard for the kiddies;
    ditto the kiddies for us –
    malice reciprocal, dread.]

'Outraged of Telford' has written to
tell the Editor how, last
    Saturday, she and her spouse
    went to the Precinct to shop.

There was 'a group of young teenagers
lounging round in a doorway'
    spawling and picking their spots.
    One, a girl aged about 12,

moved from her mates to the side of the
old chap (husband of 'Outraged'),
   where she took hold of his arm,
   disgorged her pink bubble-gum,

said to him 'What do you think of the
youth of Telford, eh, sexy?'
   'Not very much', he replied,
   shaking her free of his arm.

Whereupon she became violent,
spat phlegm into the man's face,
   screamed 'Well I'll tell you what, cunt,
   we think *you're* old fucking shits!'

('Outraged of Telford' has written it
c dash t, for discretion;
   similarly f dash g;
   similarly s dash t.)

[As I have elsewhere remarked, these are
times which baffle the oldies –
   wee kiddiwinkies infest,
   parricide, parricide soon...]

   [This isn't elegy but
   thanksgiving; therefore invert –
place the pentameter first and the
hymn/hexameter after.]

   April – the Met. Office says
   warmest since records began.
Pure cerulean of sky and, be-
hind the cottage, thick-fleeced ewes

   suckle robust new Clun lambs,
   celandines gleam from sunned turf,
first of the season's *Phylloscopus*
warblers *hweet* from the pleached thorn,

primrose – [enough of this crap.
Sounds like the Plashy Fen School.
No *list* of species can ever be
more than gross insult to them –

patronised tweely by bards
(awfully keen on Wild Life)].
I shall confine myself merely to
bringing forth a scrubbed table,

setting it down in lush grass,
placing rich wallflowers, just cut,
fumous of uncloying honey, and
to the business of olives,

watercress, paprika, rice,
breaking moist pizza apart
(anchovies, capers and sharp oreg-
ano bruised into fragrance),

sloshing out goblets of light
sap-green cool Tokay d'Alsace,
cascading Vichy, bright sparkle of
glassfuls frosted to fjord-cold...

[All he could do was *report*
horrible and (some) nice things.]
There is an impotent gratitude
goes with godless well-being.

Elsewhere, the world is to-cock;
here though, quite simply, this hour
glows as amongst the most joyful (old-
fashioned word) in a short life.

Mr Mugabe had kindly ar-
ranged a Government tour for
   journalists, that we might see
   with our own eyes and report

how Ndebele tribe villagers
had *not* suffered abuses
   from his nice CIO* men
   (30 of whom came along,

armed to the teeth, with us then as a
guard of honour, unwanted),
   how allegations were 'False,
   spread by alarmists and foes'.

This Ndebele supports oppos-
ition leader Nkomo;
   get my drift, see what I mean?
   Witnesses, then, were few/brave.

One Dr Devee reported how
he had treated a hundred
   patients who said they were raped,
   beaten or had their kin shot.

One Ndebele explained how he
watched troops gun down his brother
   whom they had forced to help dig,
   screaming for mercy, his grave.

One witness said 'I am not afraid –
there are too many have been
   beaten and, yes, that includes
   small babies on women's backs.

Six were shot dead by the soldiers – I
know, I handled the bodies.'
   (CIO officers took
   photographs of this young man;

* Zimbabwe PM Robert Mugabe's Central Intelligence Organisation.

maybe they paid him a social call
later on in the evening.)
  Witnesses showed us a wood
  where there were two mounds of earth.

These, they alleged, were the places where
six men, killed by Mugabe's
  troops, had been piled in a tump
  roughly gone over with dirt...

Villagers In Matabeleland
Tell Of Killing & Rape By –
  [Who wants to dwell on it all?
  Nil Carborundum, OK?

What after Elegy? Callous de-
tatchment feigning concern for
  Post-Elegiac and Post-
  Post-Elegiac *H. sap*...

Shake off those gloomy and old-fangled
boring, sad Elegiacs!
  Try our own new-look re-vamped
  Alcmanic Strophe, wherein

  form, ham-philosophy, alcoholism
  may not *transcend*, but do celebrate simply
  just Going On, Getting On With It. Try our
fun Catalectic Tetrameter, with Hexameter added!]

These are the days of the horrible headlines,
Bomb Blast Atrocity, Leak From Reactor,
Soccer Fans Run Amok, Middle East Blood Bath,
PC Knocks Prisoner's Eye Out In Charge Room.
Outside, the newsvendors ululate. Inside,
lovers seek refuge in succulent plump flesh,
booze themselves innocent of the whole shit-works.
Why has the gentleman fallen face-forward
into his buttered asparagus, Garçon?
He and his girlfriend have already drunk two
bottles of Bollinger and they were half-tight
when they arrived at the place half-an-hour since.
Waiters man-handle the gentleman upright,
aim him (with smirks at the lady) towards his
quails (which he misses and slumps in the gravy –
baying, the while, for 'Encore du Savigny').
He is supplied with the Beaune, which he noses,
quaffs deeply, relishes... sinks to the gingham
where he reposes susurrantly. There is
'63 Sandeman fetched to revive him.
Chin on the Pont l'Evêque, elbow in ash-tray,
as from the *Book of the Dead*, he produces
incomprehensible hieroglyphs, bidding
Access surrender the price of his coma
unto the restaurateur, kindly and patient.
These are the days of the **National Health Cuts**,
days of the end of the innocent liver;
they have to pay for it privately, who would seek anaesthetic.

['There is a Madness abroad, and at home the
cities run bloody with Riot; my children,
know yourselves happy who, far from base Commerce,
plough your own acreage. Pray for all Statesmen.
Though we had nothing to do with them, we must
suffer for Sins of our sires...' My poor flock will
be unaware of Horatian echoes
when I deliver this to them on Sunday –
two or three scarcely forbearing to slumber.
There is a Madness abroad – in Retirement only, is Saneness.]

Sweet-voicèd holy-tongued maidens [quoth Alcman],
My limbs can no longer carry me. Would that
I could go, be as the Kingfisher who doth
Go with his mates on the flower of the billow,
Height of foam having rejoicing heart sea-dark bird very sacred!

[Far from the clash of arms, having the cure of
Claresmould-cum-Cowperly, all I can hope is
these humble fragments translated may lighten
some reader's heart, as my own is disburthened
daily engaging in, if futile, harmless
little unhurtful things. So, 'My Dear Lockhart...
whether the Lyrica Graeca here Englished
may be of interest to "Quarterly" readers...
Sir, I remain yr. most...' There is a Madness currently rampant.]

Has been ordainèd three seasons, the Summer,
Winter, and Autumn the third one, and fourthly
Spring when things sprout or are lush but one can not,
You can not, it is not possible that one,
Eats to or feeds to satiety, fullness...
These words and song were invented, composed by,
Alcman-found, putting together the prolix,
Chattering noisiness utterance of some
Partridges...[There is a Madness abroad and elsewhere confusion.

Madness abroad. Through the Parsonage casement,
(cawing for carrion) crows; from the stable,
audible hiss of the groom at the pale roan;
moan of the ancient yew under whose umbrage
rest the dear bones of my good predecessors.
Ah, but, odds-heartikins! How late the hour – the Up Mail already!]

I don't know quite how it come about, but that
night I was utterly pissed as a – well I'd
been on the bottles of Special since half-past
five when they opened and then a few whiskies.
All I remember is puking and then the Hurry-Up-Waggon.

It was the usual set-up of two rough
blankets, a mattress and bog in the corner
(stunk of stale piss cos the flusher was nackered),
normal graffiti scratched on the green bedstead,
'Coppers is bastards' was wrote and I added
'Just do your bird like a man and stop moanin.'
If you stood up on your toes you could just see
through the bars over the yard to the charge room's clock on the
green wall.

Then I hears this bloke what come in with my batch,
pissed he was, also like, screamin and screamin
'You've knocked my eye out!' and 'Why have you done this?'
They done the copper what done it at Southwark –
I had to go and give evidence (I got
pissed as a rat for the Hell of it, after that little session).

Aping the brash U.S. varsities, silly
Regional Arts men are buying the local
poetry-wallah's Rough Manuscript Draft Sheets –
'Rough Drafts' belong in the wastepaper-basket
(one might as well propose purchasing Fleming's dirty old test-tubes).

dear sir and Maderm

I thought I would write as
not wrote for SOME TIME account of the ILLNES
What with the Gennal Electioned and suchlike
Voting the various Pollertics peoples
me and the husband has gone to the pole – well
ought to go shouldn't you as it is RIGHTS like
only I must say you wonder like sometimes
why they wont do what the voters are wanting.
such as no war and more Schools and the Pension.
my man has WUOND from the last which is horrid
only he say they should BAN the atomics
as it is FUTIL he say, but we dont know
being just voters which isnt the same as
Guverning which is for those who are GOOD BRAINS
out of the BIG unerversity College
but it seem sometimes the pollertick MPs
does not do Sensible things like to spend on
Aerocraft MISILS that kill some poor peoples
where they are DROP. but we only are voters
which, cannot KNOW like the Goverment peoples
what is for best but American peoples
seems to be feared at the RUSSHA invadings
so we must have them. the Rockits. but sometimes
maybe I wonders and so does the HUSBAND
what will INVADING FORS get if it comes here?
what with no money for SCHOOL or the old folks?
only we cannot know what they are thinking.
MPs and suchlikes PRY MINISTERS as they
KNOW more than we do. so <u>must</u> be the leaders
therefor we just do the best we can manige
Only the SON who the police is arrested
who is GOOD LAD but they say he is MUGGER
oh dear I do not know which way to turn but
still love my boy who is GOOD BOY to Mother
even if crimaly wrong to the lawyers
How to stop vilence and crime and the warfair
that is the questions what faces the whole WORLD
goverments nowdays and what is the answer
I dont know nor does the HUSBAND we only
have to get on with it just GOING ON is

all we can do in the present sitution
which is why I do the Cleaning for people
so that the husband which CANT WORK account of
wuond from LAST WAR that is v. painful sometimes
also the kiddies can live and be happy
even the one that is jailed (when he come out)
he must be looked after even though some say
he is bad boy. I say I am the MOTHER
so I must love him like all the worlds peoples
even if sometimes is HORRIBLE must make BEST OF A BAD JOB

hoping it finds you as leave me Yrs Faithly. VIV keep yr chin up!

When they were chasing the 'Most Wanted Gunman',
every day everyone looked in the paper
(Elsie, the barmaid, used always to leave the
Sun on the counter for regulars) and we
all there considered that he was a bastard –
dangerous bastard who wouldn't mind using
guns on the police or the public, a nutter.
'Sooner they ration that bastard to H.M. porridge the better.'

Everyone knew him to be a prize bastard
'Bloody good job' I remarked to the Lounge when
plain-clothes-men cornered him down in the Tube and
all of us then if we'd half a chance would have
strung-up the dangerous lunatic dirty bastard but, mind you,

25 years is a terrible
prospect, if you love someone.
They believe he was obsessed
with getting back to his girl

(can't blame him, either, for that – she was
very sexy the *Sun* said).
He wrote her desperate notes
like: 'All I have now is death…

take away pain of my not being
with you' that sort of garbage.
'What ever death is, it can't
be worse than waiting for you.'

Cold in his T-shirt and underpants
with a piece of electric
flex from a fridge round his neck;
desolate poor little bloke.

This is unclean: to eat turbots on Tuesdays,
tying the turban unclockwise at cockcrow,
cutting the beard in a south-facing mirror,
wearing the mitre whilst sipping the Bovril,
chawing the pig and the hen and the ox-tail,
kissing of crosses with peckers erected,
pinching of bottoms (except in a yashmak),
flapping of cocks at the star-spangled-banner,
snatching the claret-pot off of the vicar,
munching the wafer without genuflexion,
facing the East with the arse pointing backwards,
thinking of something a little bit risqué,
raising the cassock to show off the Y-fronts,
holding a Homburg without proper licence,
chewing the cud with another man's cattle,
groping the ladies – or gentry – o'Sundays,
leaving the tip on the old-plum-tree-shaker,
speaking in physics instead of the Claptrap,
failing to pay due obeisance to monkeys,
loving the platypus more than the True Duck,
death without Afterlife, smirking in Mecca,
laughing at funny hats, holding the tenet
how that the Word be but fucking baloney,
failing to laud the Accipiter which Our Lord saith is Wisdom.

Started by *Australopithecus*, these are
time-honoured Creeds (and all unHoly doubters
shall be enlightened by Pious Devices:
mayhems of tinytots, low-flying hardwares,
kneecappings, letterbombs, deaths of the firstborns,
total extinctions of infidel unclean wrong-godded others).

Atheist bigoted bad taste...[well, yes but,
unlike the worst of the killing religions,
this doesn't seek to do physical harm to other-believers.]

Smugly it advocates going on sanely
tendering love at a personal level...
[yes, there's a smugness and paradox to that
love which discriminates Sweetheart and Swinehound;
'Love me, love my madness' – non-acquiescent embracing, it
should be.]

This is the verse of negation and sterile
rage; the ironic/sarcastic declines to
nihilist cynical mute acquiescence...
[nihilist, certainly, so it is. But to
recognise isn't to acquiesce. Sterile, angry the *OIMOI*!]

Green-painted steel truckle, mattress besmirched with
previous occupants' greasy exudings
(2 blankets ditto), unflushable toilet
smelling (like privet flowers) sickly of urine,
unctuous phlegm-green wall, floor of smoothed concrete,
meshed fenestration, unfunctioning bell-push,
ferric inspection-plate slid tight in oiled slots.

Lysosomes, ribosome, sac, cytoplasm,
sausage-shaped small mitochondria, membrane,
smooth endoplasmic reticulum (lipid
molecules), globular ribosomes on the
rough endoplasmic reticulum (proteins),
nucleus storing genetic instruction
programmed in deoxyribonucleic...

[Inside the cramped cell, the coded graffito:
Just do your bird like H. sap *without moaning*.]

[Letter to Lockhart: '...Alcmanium Metrum
may be of interest to "Quarterly" readers;
and I must hope that "The Scorpion" shall not
look with disfavour upon these slight, Englished,
little, unhurtful things. Sir, I remain yr...']

I know the Laws (or the musical modes or
Strains or the customs) of all of the winged tribe.

Ah, it is not Aphrodite but manic
Eros who plays at the games which a child will –
Caning a-down on the tips of the flowers,
Blooms of the sweet-smelling Cyperus *marsh plant;*
And do not, blooms of this, contact or touch me!

Peaks and the clefts of the mountains are sleeping,
Headlands and torrents, and crawling tribes (which are
Fed by the loamy black), animals of the
Mountain and race of the bees and the brute-beasts
Inside the deeps of the purple sea. They sleep
Also the tribes of extended attenuated or long-wings.

[Theme for the sermon at Claresmould o'Sunday:
'...visit the sins of the fathers upon the...
unto the third and the fourth generation...'
There is, odds-boddikins!, madness abroad, and
something horrendous seems likely to happen,
newspaper print blackens palms with the world's dirt,
Terrible Lizards* are being awoken –
daily the saurian monsters are raised and Genesis threatened.

All I can hope is for solace in these poor impotent strophes.]

* The nomenclature *Dinosauria* was established at the 1841 Plymouth meeting of the British Association for the Advancement of Science.

There is a reciprocity here of maniac malice.
Theists are butchers, and twerpish their god-loves,
vicious PC punches prisoner's eye out,
Angels euphorically slaughter their buddies,
some PMs have Special Men to do-in your
Mrs or nipper or you if you vote wrong,
kiddies are calling us cunts and will kill us,
addle-brained Counter-revs. maim all and sundry,
man sets to work on his neighbour with rip-saw,
horrified mum watches mugger stab tot blind,
niggers are here to be murdered in season,
OAP women are here to be fucked with lavatory brushes,
my little baby annoys me – I burn it, punch off the blisters.

[Bit of a habit, the feigned indignation,
various metres, Alcmanics and so forth,
ludic responses to global débâcles.
Just Going On remains possible through the
slick prestidigital art of Not Caring/Hopelessly Caring.]

Half-batty Writer-in-Residence meets the
totally lunatic amateur hopefuls
gathered in Scumton Community Centre
proffering Fictional Openings e.g.

(1)

I won't forget in a hurry the time Young
Master came home on a Saturday *sober*:
dog didn't know him and bit him, the old mare
whinnied and cast off a shoe, and the Mistress
swooned clean away at the novelty of it.

(2)

Sappy, the Last Man, was whistling Nielsen's
4th when his dungarees started to smoulder.

[**Poets' & Novelists' Surgery** – ballocks.
Still, I suppose, if it keeps them from other, more harmful mischief...]

Ten million million kilometres are 1
light year (approx.), and at 2 1/4
million light years lies the most distant object
dimly apparent to *sapiens* vision
i.e. Andromeda Galaxy (nearby
M33 is at 2.4 million
light years, but only perceptible given ideal conditions).

You no love Elephant, Islam, Jehovah?
You no love Christ, Kakistocracy, Kali?
You no love Crapicrap Mightiest Monkey?
You no bow down to the Moon, to the UFO?
You no love balderdash? You no love daft hats?
You no love thuribles? [You no love puny
arrogant cowardly grasping at transcendentalist bunkum?]
We send you envelopes full of our faeces.
We send you Jiffy bags – blow-up your faces.
We send the tanks and the rockets [because the
Prophet saith blast us to buggery, in his Infinite Wisdom].

Here are the frail astronomically puny
half way through ten billion years of a sun life –
four million tonnes of its matter per second
warming them/cooling it. All suns collapsing,
dense cores imploding towards tiny compact
white dwarfs or neutron stars, pulsars or black holes.
Frail astronomical punies who need not
further exacerbate grim molestations
already programmed in impartial light years,
cosmic vicissitudes, cooling expansion;
no need to bugger *each other* up further –
all hands susceptible anyway to thc old astral physics.

You got a purse full of dollars and me not.
You got a mansion with stuff in what I want.
You like the football team what isn't my one.
You wear the scarf what is not the right colours.
You got a body not want me to stuff it.
You ugly oldster got pension. Me take it.
Smash in your faces with head-butts and crowbars.
Rip down your knickers at knife-point and snatch it.
Splinter the bottles and slash till the blood comes.
[Dominant morphisms hatch on the terraces dripping with apes'
gore.]

My work is closely allied to the 'Double
Quasar' (so-called) at some 10 000 million
light years from this planet. Like many quasars,
this has a couple of radio lobes which
stretch out some one hundred thousand, or so, light
years. It's a more or less average quasar,
lying, I say, at some 10 000 million light years away from

Don't get excited about it – it's only
updated *Australopithecus* and you
can't talk about it (or be it) without ac-
cepting what characterises a species,
can't profess fondness or caring for *it* ab-
stract from its coded behavioural special characteristics.

That's what they are, the old daft superstitious
killing religions and butcherous greedy
national/personal unlovely snatchings,
sapiens attributes as are the brilliant
radiotelescopes, bio-tech, hi-tech.
(Here is invented Obscurity, wherefrom
triumphs invented Discovery; blinding
privileged Revelation where there had been no concealment.)

Love it, love its fossil skull-splitting cudgel,
love it, love its anti-tank-grenade-launcher,
love it, love its neo-pongoid theological tenets.

[Yet I persist in this unhelpful habit,
sham, atavistic, unwanted, indulgent.
Thirty-four years since the death of John Lockhart…,
still I can scarcely forbear to address him
(not that he printed my Lyrica Graeca
ever, alas, in his 'Quarterly' pages –
feeble Alcmanics I seem to recall then
proffering unto him…, equally weakly,
doubtless, these graspings at dignity through my
crude adaptation of Alcaeus' metric
into sad English beyond Elegiac…
In an old form is there dignity yet there?).
Ha! I am foundering, as is my Nation – Ocean o'erwhelms us.]

Now we must drunk and drink with a will we must,
Force or a zest since dead now is Myrsilus.
[Somehow I feel I have not captured
quite what the beautiful fragment once was.

I have derived from Alcaeus' metrical
four-line invention; twisted to travesty,
rudely reduced to dactyls, spondees,
quantity ousted by Englished stressing.]

State of the four winds I do not comprehend!
One wave is at us, rolling from gunwale there,
One from the other, we in centre,
Carried around in the black ship, hard pressed

By the great tempest; sea (or bilge) filling the
Hole for the mainmast; now all the sailcloth is
Ragged with rent holes, holy, hole-rent,
Great rips all over it, torn shards, sail-rips.

[Tum-tee-tee | tum-tum ||tum-tee-tee | tum-tee-tee
Tum-tee-tee | tum-tum ||tum-tee-tee | tum-tee-tee
Tum-tee-tee | tum-tum ||tum-tum ||tum-tum
Tum-tee-tee | tum-tee-tee ||tum-tum | tum-tum.]

Poverty: painful, also un-bearable!
Poorness is Evil, bringing great peoples down
Onto their knee-caps, kneeling, bowed down.
Comes also Helplessness, Poorness' sister.

[I am as worn, indeed, as the century.
Gone is my joy – in Crimea's carnages,
year in which Lockhart joined his Maker,
(tortuous, ánachronistic stanzas)

there fell my loins' dear fruit under Cardigan.
Blasphemous, *that* book, five autumns afterwards,
burst on us even here in Claresmould –
terribly credible, Adam ape-born.]

Jupiter drizzles; out of the Heaven comes
Great storm or tempest; streams of the waters are
Frozen-up. Cast off (strike down) tempest,
Poke the fire, mix the wine, honey'd, don't stint.

[Reverend Webb has found a new Nebula,
'N.G.C. Two Nought Two Seven'*, so he said,
earnestly, over Malmsey last night.]
Wine is man's telescope [quoth Alcaeus].

What are these birds come? Far from the (or from the
Bounds of the) Ocean? Dapple-necked, having-stripes,
Tribe of the long-wings? [Long-wings, long-wings…
Ah! But a tireful lacuna halts me.]

* NGC 7027 (not 2027) had been thought to be a star until, in 1879, the Reverend T.W. Webb discerned its slightly elongated shape. It was included in Johan Dreyer's *New General Catalogue of Nebulae and Clusters of Stars* (1888).

Reps and execs in *Plastics* and *Packaging*
(holiday-wise it's Costa del Parvenu),
Fitments and *Fords*, complete Expenses
Forms for their Beer'n'Byte basket scampi.

They are disgusting; I am a secular
saint of the breed Empiricist Atheist
(here is a quid for Oxfam hapless
starving in sewer-pipes somewhere beastly).

There was a scuffle and shouts on the
station concourse and then they
ran out and I heard a knife
drop on the floor and three men

ran off and there was a terrified
Rastafarian lying
bleeding like mad from the chest.
Railway men gave him first aid

but he continued to bleed from a
gaping gash in the rib cage.
Gently I rested his frizzed
head in my arm like a girl's.

One of the officers taking my statement
said how he died in the hospital later,
how he was wanted for mugging, and not to
waste too much sympathy brooding on someone
equally capable, probably, of the same sort of slaughter.

Being thus fully conscious of hideous
qualities in us (knowing these qualities,
merely specific, are not 'special'
other than to ourselves) does not mean an

overall hate for, nor acquiescence in,
sapiens wholesale. Even its butcherous
lunatic scum is (oimoi!) part it –
love it (with its bloody cleaver)/loathe it.

Media elbow-deep in the offal-bin
(Flensed-Alive MPs Mangled In Bomb-Attack),
nincompoop zealots toy with jelly,
Crass Kakistocracies viva, viva...

Moisturise lungs with juice of the vinous-bred,
Sirius rises, now is the difficult
Season of hardness, all are thirsty
Out of the terrible heat the hotness.

Grasshopper (sweetly) goes into mourning, now
Makes an annoying sound from the foliage;
Artichoke now is thornful blooming,
Women are utterly most foul, ghastly

Tribe of Mankind is impotent (delicate,
Helplessly unpeeled, wasted to weakliness),
Sirius parches, not just head but
(Organs of genesis) knee-caps also.

But let there be a garland of aniseed
Coiling around my twisted and wrinkled neck,
Also let sweet myrrh be poured over
Onto my (over our) chest or bosom.

[Garnering remnants, fossilised, civilised,
I, mealy-mouthed disruptor of harmonies,
strive in an old form (not strong, mayhap),
cunningly structural – weekly helpful?]

Husband ye not one plant of the bushy tribe
First-before (or in) preference to the vine!
[Sanity is a feeble weapon
set against lunacy, nobly helpless.]

STET

(1986)

Pyrex, a pie-dish, deep-lined with apple lumps,
deft in the left hand; with the right, flopping on
pall of white-dusted droopy pastry,
slicing off overlaps, jabbing steam-vents...

'52: Mummy paused, wiped a floured hand and tuned in the wireless –
sad Elgar, crackling, then *death of our King, George the Sixth.*

'Wrote to Miss Prudence, you know at *Comfy Home*
"Time will heal all wounds wonderful" *she* says
"No need to av flowers nless yer wants em.
Yer can wear black if yer wants to" *she* says.'

Engines cut out, thick snow dumbed harmonious
doves numbed in frozen postures of flight and we
found in the eerie too-bright morning
rhubarb leaves crusting the ice-whorled window.
Those at the bank and the grocer's are that peculiar fetial
brand of perniciousness which wars and cold climates produce.

Muse!, sing the Grotty [scant alternative].

Cro-Magnon, simian, Neanderthal,
whom Mr Justice Russell sentences
to 46 years (total) for assault
on Mr Harry Tipple and his wife...

Charles Bradford, Terence Bradford, Edward Mitchell,
broke into Mr Tipple's corner shop.
After they had assaulted him he had
black eyes, a broken nose, bruised lacerated
torso and face and buttocks. He had his head
banged on the floor and had his feet stamped on.
He was knocked senseless with a bottle. Cans
of aerosol paint and fly-spray were fizzed up
his nose and mouth. Bradford and Mitchell next
started to cut his ear off, but then hacked
off Tipple's toe with a serrated knife.
The toe was then stuffed into Tipple's mouth
(playing *This Little Piggy* on the kid's
little pink blobs is not so much fun now).

And Mrs Tipple croodles in the box
as she explains how both her eyes were blacked,
her nose was broken, she was 'in the most
humiliating and degrading way'
indecently assaulted by the men –
one of whom 'used a knife in an obscene
bizarre vile filthy ithyphallic manner'.
Charles Bradford, Terence Bradford, Edward Mitchell,
before they left the Tipples bound and gagged,
turned, faced them, and, unzipping, each produced
his member and pissed long and copiously
into the faces of the hapless pair.

An acned trio lowers from the front page.
Cro-Magnon, simian, Neanderthal
(but the same species as Christ, Einstein, Bach).

[Trite impotent iambic journalese,
Reading Raps Raiders/Poet Pete Protests.]

[Re-draft the sick obsessional chuntering,
strike out the old gratuitous cruelties...
(re-draft be buggered, leave as printed,
Hail!, uncorrectable Age of Floored Proofs).]

When (early '60s?) there was an influx of
collared doves spreading rapidly through the realm,
monthly we mapped the species' progress
(hanging for murder was being phased out –

noosed necks diminished/proliferated in inverse ratio),
dubbed it the Year of the Noose; unforeseen increase ensued.

Obsolete bivalves of the Silurian
scutter from flaked rock onto a Viva squashed
in the Scrap Merchant's disused quarry
(lugged in on Saturday – bad do, A5).

We went to see it that evening; bashed-in badly, the near-side.
Mangled up into the roof, strands of maroon-stained blonde hair.

and it is these hydrogen atoms' radio emissions to which I refer. The wavelength at which hydrogen atoms radiate is, of course, 21.106 centimetres, and when I tune the scope to this wavelength, what I am able to record is static hydrogen – neither moving towards nor away from us.

And if you wish to 'observe' advancing or retreating clouds containing this interstellar gas?

Well, if I re-tune to 21.105 centimetres, then I am able to record clouds that are moving towards us at a velocity of 50 000 kilometres per hour. If I retune to 21.107 centimetres, then I am able to record clouds which are moving away at the same velocity.

This 'Hydrogen Line' was predicted, was it not, by Hendrick van de Hulst, the Dutch astronomer, during the war, and first detected in 1951?

Correct. And, of course, there are other radio emissions from other materials in space, detectable at different wavelengths – for example, the first molecule found in space by my colleague in 1963, a water molecule minus one hydrogen atom, (OH), hydroxyl, radiates at a wavelength of 18 centimetres. But most molecules radiate at the shorter, often submillimetre, wavelengths bordering on the far infra-red.

And what of your own particular concerns?

Yes, well, I've no interest whatsoever in our local system, in isolation. My concern is the very furthest reaches, where the colossal explosions of the quasars are faintly

[Bellicose *H. sap.*] Skull-cleaving Harriers,
distant a field before their ventriloquous
        stridencies strip dense gold male flowers,
                hedge-hop me pruning the *Quercus ilex*.

Valorous, some of them, homicides all by grey acquiescence.
    Holm sap is smeared and it smells bitterly on the poised blade.

'53: gleeful, briskly we marched from the
Infants to see the New Coronation and
Everest Conquered, double feature,
into a gaudily faded *Regal*.

Tenzing and Hillary flickering, last real British achievement/
shock of the shot of our new Monarch sat *twiddling its thumbs!*

When the daft queen came to Bootle the crowd stank sweat-rank
and squashed me;
scuffers controlled it – I liked [still do] Law more than the Mob.

I thank you kindly sir! Bitter and mild mixed.
Like I was saying like, once they gets in like,
you know to Parlerment, hear no more of em.
Taxes and that like and where's it all going?
Not to the pensioners any road, mister.
Same with the kids in the schools an that now see,
parents has got to ave whip-rounds and that like –
pay for the stuff as the kids use in school like.
Course when the Goverment sees as it's able
not to spend taxes on kids' educations,
they cuts the school money more see – they knows like
how the old parents'll have a whip-round like.
Same with the Health Service money and that like,
Goverment knows as the public'll whip-round
so as to get what the hospitals need like.
That's what the Goverment wants cos the private
patients is all right and others has whip-rounds –
pay for the hospital stuff as is needed.
Therefore the Goverment don't have to pay for
schools and the Health Service so there's more tax for nucular
warflair.

Probably merely twinge of dyspepsia,
nothing at all, just tremulous tightness to
left of the sternum, absolutely
peak of condition and body tip-top,

stick to the Perrier more in the future, high fibre diet,
jogging, longevity, yes, jogging, longevity, yes.

Esther Albouy was twenty-one years old
when the war ended, and she was denounced,
by neighbours in her village in the Auvergne,
for fraternising with a German soldier.
She had her head shaved in the Public Square.
Her parents, who were overcome with shame,
then locked her in her room, letting her out
only at night, occasionally, on a leash.
When, after twenty years, her parents died,
she could not bear to face the outside world.
No one had seen her go outside the house
for thirty-eight years.

1983:
some Carmelite nuns managed, at last, to get
an eviction order for a house they owned
where no rent had been paid for many years
by the occupants – an old woman recluse
and her two brothers.

The *Gendarmerie*
had to use gas-masks when they forced their way
into the house, so overpowering was
the stench from filth and a green rotting corpse
(one of the brothers died three years before).
The gas and water had been long cut off.

She and her one surviving brother, whom
she slept in the same bed with, were removed
into a psychiatric hospital,
tenir en laisse, so she is pleased to think.

[Strike out the old obsessional nastiness,
justify, take out all the extraneous,
    PRINTER, insert rule, take back, wrong fount,
        change damaged character(s), strike out error...]

La bouche amère, cru gâté, sécheresse.

My sole concern is unmoving hydrogen
(Hydrogen Line predicted by van de Hulst)
    bunched between distant stellar clusters,
        tuned into 21.106...
        [Let it stand; Reasonless causal physics.]

['McDonald (Mrs), Aberdeen' is adjudged
winner of Poem of the Week.]

Dirty sex violence of TV
    Should never be allowed
No wonder we can see
    The badly-behaved crowd!
Och! They will be punished
    On the Judgement Day,
Before the Lord is finished
    They will rue the day!
These do-gooder social workers
    Saying 'Let them go free'
Are all sinful shirkers
    Sent by Satan 'gainst you and me.

The way to stop these hooglums
   At football match or fight
Is string them up by thumbs
   Until they can tell Right
From Wrong, then ways of Jesus
   Will get into their heart
Which, at the present, freezes
   And they know not where Love starts.

'Gie im a pint quick – diggin is grave wi is
prick e is, this bloke: seen im on Satdy night
      parked in the Quarry, winders steamed-up,
            flattened them oats o mine, randy fuckerrr.'

A bloke with whom I once worked at the mill,
one bait-time, in the Bait-Room, peeled the lid
back from his Tupper sandwich-box, produced
two off-white thick amorphous slabs of bread
wherefrom a pinkish greyish matter oozed.
He bit, considered, rolled blear red-veined eyes,
spat an envenomed mouthful on the floor,
hurled the offending bait-box to his feet
(Terpsichoreans might have found the way
he rain-danced it to smithereens beneath
steel-toe-capped boots inspired, original),
then opined 'Fucking stupid bloody cow!
Wait till I get the bitch; I'll give her *jam*
over beef dripping!' Next day he was off.
They did him (GBH?). She had to have
23 stitches – he was a big bloke.

One time, he'd been all day and half the night
hard on the piss (the Vaults and then the Club),
and on the way home stumbled against a white
new-painted door. Dismayed, he bought some meths
down at the late-night Chemist. In the house,
he dabbed his jacket liberally and then
fell asleep on the sofa. When his wife
came back from visiting her sister, she
found him in drunk repose reeking of meths,
the emptied bottle lying at his side.
She beat him with a heavy casserole –
dish (which had been a wedding present from
her mother, twenty-three long years before)
until the blood streamed. Some ententes rely
much on a reciprocity of malice.

Killed the apprentice – would do, a tractor tyre.
Somehow he read the pressure-gauge faultily,
kept on inflating with the air-hose.
Sounded like dynamite. Split right open.

Two decades' cobwebs were falling for nearly half an hour after;
sound-waves dislodged them – unveiled cross-members gleaming
like new.

[Don't go out there – you'll all catch your death of it,
sinister twits are in the ascendancy.
Plump up a stanza, close the brackets,
snuggle down into a cosy re-draft...]

{ Dogma-adherents,
Orthodox hirsutes, smug in eternal truth
learnt from absurd delusions of troglodytes
(*tantum religio potuit suadere malorum*)...
Heights of pernicious stupidity grow from molehills of nonsense.

I had been Crop Inspecting – C2 Pennal
which we'd provisionally bought as seed –
the eleven acres by the railway line,
and in that sheltered corner near the tunnel
someone, quite possibly in love, had been
lying. An Inter-City brayed two notes,
the Buffet car disgorged a Light Ale tin
into the especial, pseudo rural, scene:
holed Nuform, empty Long Life, laid-flat oats.

Headmaster's study: brass-knobbed Victorian
inlaid Morocco desk of mahogany,
antimacassared leather armchair,
waxy refulgence of polished volumes...

I was about 12, must have been '58,
when I was vouchsafed secular ecstasy
(some misdemeanour, farting/Lord's Prayer) –
suddenly, bruise-clouded winter evening

beamed an oblique shaft, apricot, genial,
through a grim dull pane onto the luminous
Axminster, cheery, spring-piled spectrum,
rendering misery worldly, nothing.

'Youth of today sir; never known punishment,
National Service, show em some discipline,
bring back the Birch or, like Iran has –
lectrical gedget to chop their hends orf!'

6000 acres, each hour, of rain forest
voguishly razed (at moment of going to
press) – the climactic consequences/
faunal extinctions are merely cosmic.

None of it matters except as an ego-chilling lacuna:
1.6 acres per sec... Fright = Ethical Zeal.

'3 Across: "Writer, not brave, wrote *Cavalcade*."
Tell you the truth I've only read two of his –
Portrait of Doreen Grey and that one
whatsit *The Trouble with Being Earnest*.'

Grans are bewildered by post-Coronation disintegration –
offspring of offspring of *their* offspring infest and despoil.

'54: old Miss Clio was teaching us
[genuine name, 'Miss Clio' is, by the way]
'There is no reason, is there, children,
why you can't live with other little

children from other countries in happiness?
You are the ones whom we are depending on ...'
We have betrayed her, poor old Dodo –
cleaving of crania, burnt-out Pandas...

This isn't Socrates, Einstein or Bach but just the same species
bloodily on the front page kicking itself into mulch.

'55: comics (*better* class) offered us
Decent Types it was hoped we would emulate –
Shaftesbury, Gandhi, Dickens, Florence
Nightingale, Faraday, Curie, Elgar...

'85: some of us clearly have been more moved by the *worse* ones –
Bloody-Nosed Basher, The Yobbs, Sheik Fist The Middle East
Nit...

All in this place anticipate the Dreadful.

[The weak theatrical one-liner whine
before the scalpel. How to justify
expatiation? Call it a day at that.]

Bad dégustation; puant the cru, short, séché the finish.

At the 1985 Royal Naval Equipment Exhibition in Portsmouth, is a set of six gold-plated Sterling Mark IV submachine guns, each with 12 gold-plated 9mm bullets. Complete with magazine and bayonet, displayed in a walnut case, each costs £9,000. 'Ordered by a foreign construction company for Royalty', discloses the righteous (all those juicy jobs!) Sterling Co. of Dagenham, Essex.

Marvellous boost to British Economy...
thousands of jobs created in Armaments...
unemployed needy welcome new hope...
Export Achievement and can't you see that

had not Great Britain landed this wonderful
order for Saudi R.A.F. fighter planes,
[hordes of *Tornado* urbane zappers]
some other nation would soon have stepped in...

benefit to the needs of our own people...
Government not responsible... actions of
leaders of other... thus Great Britain's
Satrapess gloatingly self-applauding.

Another exhibit is a fast patrol vessel built by Souters of Cowes, Isle of Wight, for the Bahrain Navy.

Inside the 100ft vessel, the bridge roof is lined with grey suede and the public rooms smell of the fresh opulence of their cream leather seating.

Blue carpets cover the decks, and the best German furniture and equipment fills the galley.

The bathrooms are lined with royal blue marble, there is a sunken bath, the toilet bowls are of smoked glass, the taps are of 22 carat gold.

The master bedroom features an oval bed, the television and video rise from the floor and smoked glass mirrors line the walls. A Danish hi-fi system pipes music throughout.

A 20 millimetre gun and an anti-aircraft missile system are carried.

Accommodation for the crew of 15 is squashed into the forecastle, cramped bunks 18 inches apart.

The Bahrain Navy has paid £1.7 million for this Wasp class boat to be used by a 'very senior minister' of the tiny Gulf sheikdom.

'56: going home from the Juniors,
I read the headlines **Suez** and **Crisis Point** –
crikey! I thought, there must be something
terribly wrong with the nation's toilets;

soon if the Government didn't act there'd be all kinds of nasties
gushing up out of the drains, Britain would be [is] engulfed.

[The Editor is moved to publish *Not As Bad As All That* by 'Contented of Telford, Mrs']

I count my blessings every day
   And night before I go to bed,
A little 'Thank You' prayer I say
   On going to bed.
Because Our Lord has given me
   Two good strong legs and arms
I am not handicapped you see
   And eyesight to see His charms
Like the bright-coloured flowers
   And the bright blue of the sky
And Dame Nature's flowry bowers
   Quiet where I can lie.

This world is not as bad as all that
   In spite of the strikes and wars
And football violence and all that
   And mugging and 'Nature red in claw'.
So to Our Lord a praise I sing
   To thank Him for this life
That pleasures like a cup of tea can bring
   And my dear children and being a wife.

Fossil Silurian crinoids infest our cottage's walls of
   local stone; thin plasterboard separates them from ourselves.

Don't get me wrong now mate, just half in there thanks.
I thank you kindly sir! Don't get me wrong now.
I know we got to have army defences,
otherwise have bleeding lunatics step in,
then look out mister like that Ayertolly
you know or commies or some of them others –
all bleeding lunatics, L-O-N-U-T –
forcing the people to do what they say like.
That is Dictatorships, no one wants that mate.
So there has got to be forces defences.
Mind you I don't say I holds with this bleeding
nucular warflair, don't hold with it me mate.
Too much of that bleeding lot an we all be
dead as a yo-yo mate. Bitter and mild please.
Same with them low-flying Harriers what they
trains off the Air-Base as deafens you almost
zoomin like that about twenty feet up like,
fetch all the blossom all off of the trees mate
with the vibration and that you know. They got
nucular bombs as they fires out of them mate.
Too much that nucular lot and we all be
dead as a yo-yo mate. Let it stand, I say. Dead as a yo-yo.

[Non-acquiescent acknowledgement; present but muted the ***OIMOI!***]

Very Long Baseline Interferometry
renders the quasar 3C 273
(2000 million light years distant)
clearly discernible – my sole interest...
[Stet; Ave!, Reasonless causal physics.]

Impasse of US/USSR has stopped
dangerous hate-states getting too uppity.
        Volunteer acned cannon-fodder
                (unemployed school-leavers, while supplies last)

    keeps yellow oldies like me free from conscription. To these:
generous History, Geography, Stalemate, I am most grateful.

A lady's album of 1826
in my possession, contains the following
one-liner alexandrine unexplained:

Something ridiculous & sad will happen soon.

Top of the sequence: washer-shaped crinoid stalks/
brachiopods in layered Silurian
        delvings of Wenlock Limestone quarry
                disused except by the yokel neatherds

digging their graves with their pricks after late-night Saturday
        piss-ups –
    dark Vivas parked emit moans, Fetherlites pile up in shales.

'Sensitive things them Topical Rain Forests,
regulates all the Global Humility,
        neccitates Nature Conversation,
                otherwise animals Mass Distinction.'

Beadily, sloes still hang under midwinter
snow (a kind summer, autumn and freezing have
    increased the fructose level somewhat),
        sweeten a withering palate, slightly.

['Contented of Telford, Mrs' submits her poem
Faith to the Editor.]

All this terrible rape and murder
    And mugging and violence galore
And poor little children beaten
    Oh! my heart can stand no more.
There is always someone on strike
    For better pay and terms,
Is there no end of this misery?
    No one ever learns.
But before despair descends
    Upon my sad head
A name crops up in the paper
    And I no longer wish I was dead!
I'm filled with fresh, new hope,
    I'm certain that Billy Graham,
With words of Truth and Love,
    Will bring an end to this horrid mayhem.

[Don't let the Old Ineluctable catch you with your clichés down –
Cope with No Hope without god./Recognise, not acquiesce.]

When I was sacked from Uncle Chummy's Mail
(formerly Uncle Chummy's Letterbox)
for being tight – don't mind my telling you? –
I got the *Comfy Home's* Miss Prudence page –
Problems and all that bilge, and Poetry.
'An incident occurred whereby some s * * * m
got in my mouth and then I swallowed it.
Can you get pregnant like this?' 'Do not fear,
my young friend, I enclose some National Health
leaflets...' and it goes on and on and on.

The Poem of the Week slot (10 quid prize)
helps boost a meagre salary – 'Content
of Telford, Mrs' wins most frequently,
or dour 'MacDonald (Mrs), Aberdeen'
('I'm really sure Our Lord and Billy Graham
Will put an end to all this horrid mayhem',
'To football hooglums' [sic] 'will come a day
When they repent that they have gone astray');
I chuck the other pratts straight in the bin –
hundreds of poor sad losers every week.

Creamy-pink curled tongues speckled with pollen dust:
slightly vanilla edge and the syrupy
 blend in the fumes of honeysuckle,
 cleanly, deliciously sweet, uncloying.

This, and dusk fragrance of hay (most of the field has been
 cropped)
mingle as, nosing the cru, we remark its generous finish.

Mixed mild and bitter – I thank you sir, kindly!
Haven't I been proper rotten with flu like?
Rotten with flu I been, all this week, I have.
Been in bed all the week, missed the old voting –
you know, the polling like, having the flu like.
Not as a vote off me'd make any change like.
Fixed they am, all the same, all the same them lot.
Once they gets Parlerment, hear no more of em.
This is it, this is it – speak as I find, me.
Speak as I find I does, all the same them lot.
Him as is standing's just same as them others.
End up no better off. Bitter and mild please.
I thank you kindly sir! You take old Churchill.
That was the feller as showed em all, Churchill.
That was the boy for the job was old Churchill.
That's what the country could do with now mister.
Industry, you know like, that's what we need like.
Soon be as dead as a yo-yo this country.
Ask me like, and I'd say dead as a yo-yo.
Soon be as dead as a yo-yo like, I'd say.
Still, that's the way as they wants it and that's the way as they'll get it.

The tramp's scalp's indigo pus-oozing boil;
sulphur dioxide piss-hued cumulus;
a mac daubed with puked Chinese take-away –
drooled noodly detail of a Jackson Pollock;
furred upside-down tench in a mauve canal...
I sing the Grotty [no alternative].

'...terribly sad news...instantly...Motorway...'
After your mother's letter I turn to a
diary, through whose Wetmore Order
ornithological recollections

stir, of a friendship early-established and
special surviving global vicissitudes.
Marvellous, those first close-shared eras
mist-netting rarities, early migrants.

[Batty/unhealthy – verse at the best of times
chunters to insubstantial minorities,
as for addressing lines to *dead men!*
arrogant therapy/piffle, claptrap.]

East and west coast observatories fêted us
(icterine and melodious warblers,
thrill of *Phylloscopus bonelli*
magnified instants of bright crisp focus)

even as that sad realm in the middle was gently expiring
devenustated but yet, even though feculent, *ours.*

[Therapy, whining, anxious to demonstrate
how the nice bard is awfully sad about
having his old pal flenched by crunched car-
others' bereavements don't marvel readers.]

25 years ago, we, at a spring's brink, tasted a chilled draught;
[Hippocrene hogwash] tonight, mawkish, I, solo, glut hock...

those days we charted our years by the dark swift coming and
going...

wants }
[Who do you think you are whining to? No reader shares } your
bereavement
and it's pathetic and mad to address yourself to the dead.]

Similar, thank you squire, bitter and mild mixed.
I thank you kindly sir! Same with them Irish
and them Iramians – that Ayertolly,
him with the whiskers like, look out for him mate.
Lunatic, he is mate, L-O-O – listen,
all the same, them lot are, mad on religion.
All them religerous lot is fernatics.
Stick all them bleeders together and let em
blow bloody buggery out of each other –
Prodestant, Catherlic, Jews Isleramics.
Whisky's no good to you mister I tell you,
Not when you're lying down, any road mister.
I been in bed for two days with the flu like,
any road, thought as I'd just have a whisky –
get me back on to me feet as they say like –
any road, straight to me kidneys it went like.
Straight to the kidneys – that's lying down, that is.
Standing's the thing like if you drinks the whisky,
by-pass the kidneys the whisky will then like.
Don't touch the kidneys at all then like, standing.
Never lie down if you're drinking the whisky.
All people got their own diffrent religions.
Obvious, that is like. Obvious, that is.
No need to kill all them others what aren't yours.
Them Sheeks with turbans on, thems just the same like.
Also them terrorists – see in the *Sun* where
that lot let off a bomb? Lunatics them mate –
L-U-N. Not to the kidneys, the *livers* –
straight to the livers and buggers em up mate.
Just half in there please squire. I thank you kindly!
All got the diffrent idees like, so we got to accept it.

The Buffet carriage lurches side to side
causing a democratic crocodile
(*Financial Timeses, Suns*, a *TES*,
spinsterly, oil-rig drunk, a see-through blouse,
two Sikhs, a briefcased First Class parvenu)
to jig like salts on storm-tossed quarterdecks.
They're queuing up to be insulted by
a truculent steward who administers
flabby cool BR toast at wondrous cost
and steaming tea in polystyrene cups
capped with thin leaky plastic lids – the car
oscillates and an old unfortunate
is scalded by spilt pekoe and then hurled
onto the carriage floor, striking her head
hard on an angle of formica counter.
A cooling tower, scrap cars bashed into cubes,
a preternaturally mauve canal.
The cut is dabbed with tissue, pronounced 'slight',
a volunteer fetches another cup,
someone produces an Elastoplast.
A Long Life shudders towards the table edge,
cramped buttocks stiffen in an orange scoop
of ergonomic fibreglass. Cropped boys
aged about sixteen, manifest recruits
(numbers and names and barracks stencilled white
on khaki kit bags), smoke, guffaw and swig.
One of their number, as a furious shepherd
might bellow some remonstrance at his dog
when it is five fields off, recalcitrant,
brays 'Ara sexy gerraknickersorf!'.
(A teenage girl of average composition,
buying a cling-filmed slice of currant cake,
stimulates this encomiastic greeting.)
Their left hands grip their right biceps, whereon
their right forearms are raised and lowered. One
pustular soldier of the Queen pretends
to grapple with an imaginary huge
phallus – his fellow-warriors are seized
with mirthful paroxysms. They all have spots
(compulsorily shaved, not left to heal)
and all read comics – caricature army,
balloons of speech exploding from the heads:

'Chuck me that Sten, I'll get the dirty dastards'.
Slight, acned raw cadets who may well be
spatchcocked in Ulster or some bloody fool
flag-waving bunkum like the Falklands do...
Company Sergeant Grit – Soldier of Stone,
Battling Burgess of the Fifty First,
Stens in the Jungle, 'Get me them grenades,
I'll show the ruddy rats how us Brits fight'...
The peaceful fields are littered with new lambs
fattening up for Easter, SO_2,
pretty canary-yellow against grey,
sweals from stark plant (the voguish acid rain),
Long Lifes vibrate, totter towards the edge.

Each time *Tornadoes* hedgehop the quarry head,
cleaving the brain-pan, tangible stridencies
judder a fossil bivalve free from
400 million years locked in matrix;

so I assumed it was these urbane killers caused the explosion
(sonic boom) but I was wrong – **TRACTOR TYRE BLOW-UP**
KILLS YOUTH.

The blushful Phillida hath been abroad –
limp 'coral' Nuform, body-shaped flat oats.

Generous Empire boldly was stencilled in
gold on a quart stone flagon converted for
use as a bedside lamp in Gran's room.
Dappling its girth was a painted world map

showing in red the bits that were under our
Sovereign's protection – much of the planet was
cheerfully daubed thus, in those gone times;
cruelty and mess, one assumed, reigned elsewhere.

Scion of large-eared risible Monarchy
serves now the useful negative function of
non-doing but of being Royal
thereby restricting all upstart PMs...

Obsolete heirloom, comforting glow of **Generous Empire**
(cruelty and mess, I suppose, may be worse elsewhere than here).

or the sheer scale of these concepts (distance, time, structural elegance governing the basic particles of which you speak) in any way determine your philosophical – one might say theological – apprehensions?

No, I don't think so – certainly not the latter. If one contemplates a so-called Grand Unified Theory of Matter, it is a system of physical causes, rather than some kind of Reason with a capital R and the implicit mumbo-jumbo of all that, which one conceives –

You are quite happy, then, with a Reasonless universe?

Oh yes. Quite happy to accept Reasonless causal physics.

Tell us about your work with VLBI.

Yes, well, in Very Long Baseline Interferometry a number of astronomers, maybe around the world, examine a common radio emission simultaneously. They keep precise track of the timings with an atomic clock – extremely accurate, you know. The tapes of their radio observations are then flown to an HQ where they're played back exactly synchronised, and they're then joined electronically. The effect is like a giant connected radio telescope.

And you 'look' at, what?

Well, my only concern is with quasars but of course this covers a huge range of phenomena. 3C 273, for example, is the nearest one to this planet (2000 million light years). But it is with rather more distant subject-matter that I'm dealing. Until recently, we knew the so-called Double Quasar as the most distant (10 000 million light years) and my colleagues at the Very Large Array in New Mexico have produced very detailed radio pictures. But we're now aware of even more remote

Just half in there please squire. I thank you kindly!
Trouble is see what the trouble is see is
diffrent religions like. All of us know like
there must be *Something* like, you know Out There like.
This can't be all there is to it like. Course not.
You know like outer space, Some One or Some Thing
must have like made it like, must be a Reason.
This is a quote like so somebody *said* it:
'Man is a very religerous creature.'
Only they got Gods as isn't the same like,
so they starts killing the ones with the wrong Gods.
No sense in that mister, no sense in that mate.
Lunatics they are mate, L-U-N, all them
Arabs and Jews and them Christian Militias,
them Irish Paisleyists, dead simple mister,
all them old Shreeks with the turban like, all dead
simple mate, lunatics. Let it stand. Loonies.
That's Uman Natur mate, soon be as bleeding dead as the yo-yo.

Somewhere in *Far East* there was a *Narmistice*
(I wasn't sure where either of these things were);
wirelesses fizzled, grown-ups seemed to
value *it* more than they did my birthday! –

I was just 7 (July 27th, '53) and the
news there would be no more war made me feel comfy inside.

to say that aftermaths *occupy your attention mainly?*

Yes, insofar as one's foci are the radio galaxies, detectable as compact-radio-source quasars, which are the indications of aftermath (in the centres of quasars, gas streams are spiralling into massive black holes). These central violent explosions throw out a couple of lobes stretching several million light years, so radio pictures show this as a kind of dumb-bell shaped emission.

Tell us about this particular one, will you?.

Yes, well, it's the remotest currently known. It's best discernible from the Parkes, Australian, radio telescope – indeed, was first picked up by that instrument. It was too remote, you know, and too far south to have been detectable by the Third Cambridge Survey, so doesn't feature in that catalogue – it was noted later in the Parkes survey. PKS 2000-330, it's classified as, and about 12 000 million light years from this planet, a

'Tell you what, old chap, *strictly* between ourselves,
I have a *leetle* personal whatsaname –
utterly *vital* I drink daily,
huge amounts, otherwise get so damn sad.'

...arrogant puny assumption that physics, uncomprehended,
must be the magic of some kind of Super-Mastermind Giant
[ham-philosophical sham-scientific atheist chunter].
Tantum religio potuit suadere malorum
(hideous Holies are hammering fuck out of other-believers).
Simple complexity, dying, euphoria, nastiness, good fun –
perfectly straightforward, no need to seek for variants of the
theisms sired by the earliest hominid terrified shamans
(cowardly greedy-weak graspings at seedy, trite consolations).
Tosh don't elucidate feeble inadequate cranial strivings.
Straightforward mystery; no need for transcendentalist hogwash.
Ave! no-nonsense astronomers probing Reasonless physics
[also the modest who just cope with No Hope, without god].

'54: old Miss Clio was teaching us
all about *Frontiers* (Asia and everywhere);
my mate's big brother, so he told me,
'died in Career for one of those things'...

when he was in the bath, you could see scars on both of Dad's
shoulders
(carrying rails for Japan) – I hated flipping Frontiers.

Crozier, coiled crook, scroll of new-sprouting green
fern at a well's brink sprung from parched mountainside.
Kneeling I sucked the silver fountain...
[Tastefully Hippocrene, verbose gobful.

Prosaically between you and the summit, hacking, appeared a
grizzled agrestic old get, wielding a bloody big scythe.]

Where my best mate lived, it was a scruffy dump
(mind you, the outside lav was a novelty),
        cockroaches scuttled – his mam called it
                'cockeroach', gaining an extra syll-thing.

Next door, the whippets shat in the scullery,
bloke used to smack his wife with a dirty old
        hessian coal-sack, called her 'fuck-pig',
                got put in jail when their baby snuffed it.

What you should do was share out the money and
make some new houses so they'd be comfy and
        teach them to wash to stop their smell and
                show them what fun it was, being humans –

once you could teach them to dislike themselves as you did, then
        clearly
things'd be smashing of course – a child of 8 could see *that*.

I edit Readers Writes (the Letters page):
'What has gone wrong with Britain since the War?',
'Ex-Soldier, Telford' asks, 'The Socialists
allowed the lower orders too much hope
by promising them radically improved
living conditions, and the dangerous
doctrine of lower-class participation –
the riff-raff started meddling in Power…'
'I blame the Immigrants', 'Housewife' opines,
'for inner-city strifes…', 'The world's gone mad!',
'Sir – Are we to assume that Western Powers
exercise no control upon their own
Military Forces? Murder has been done;
but if it suits a Military Élite
(under a Government's auspices or not)
no felon may be charged – an impotent
electorate sees its Judicature abused

by its elected leadership…', 'I heard,
distinctly, on the 4th of January,
the Cuckoo calling in St James's Park…'
Of course you can't print half of them – obscene
or batty: 'Mrs Thatcher is a cunt'
(plenty like that, whichever PM's in),
'I'd bomb the fucking wogs', 'Hanging's too good
for bastards like that' (muggers, hijackers,
people with beards, the unemployed, the child-
molesters, Hindus – everyone, it seems,
arouses someone's wrath), 'Dying's too good
for vermin like this' [so we stay alive].

A lady's album of 1826
in my possession, contains the following
pentameter one-liner unexplained:

This waiting bravely to be badly hurt

[Untrue. *You* scrawl the whining metaphor
before the scalpel, can't now justify
expatiation. Call it a day at that.]

'Unemployed/Hopeless' doesn't sufficiently
serve to explain Cro-Magnon atrocities,
vindicate *Homo troglodytes.*
Dominant morphisms wield big cudgels.

'60: I bored my mates in the 4th Form by
forecasting martial law in the larger towns –
Liverpool, Glasgow, London, Belfast,
Birmingham – nobody thought I *meant* it!

You could see, in the estates and the new slum high-rises, Morlocks
sullenly honing rank fangs; telly-taught, butcherous, brute.

'Wearing a widow's tweeds I is any road,
stiplified NO FLOWERS at the funereal,
        weighed up the mows and cons I did like,
                "Better proceed with a caution" I says.'

Demented widow lives ten years in wardrobe
when hubby croaks; one-armed volcano victim
nurses mashed tot and yowls; for some shite god,
possession, border, tenet, goons blast cack
out of each other's chitterlings... I don't care
two fucks for any other pratt. UK's
OK. I'm lucky and intend to stay so.
What do you want, me to go batty too?

Pinions veed back a peregrine stooped out of
cumulus into 2000 *canutus*
        zigzagging silver over mudflats.
                Flurry of snowy down; slate-dark scythe wings

lugged the prey westerly, do you remember? [Do you remember?
    Whom you address is now dead. Why yammer on to yourself?]

brutality }
Strike out the old obsessive mortality } ...
[Physics (unlike text) can't be corrected, though.
Let it stand. Ave! Age of Floored Proofs.
Stet (no alternative), leave as printed.]

Our land is no as bad as all that!
For when you watch TV
You see a lot of evil that
Is in many a foreign country.
For example you could take France
Who test the Atom Bomb
And lead a very merry dance
To every Harry, Dick and Tom
Who live on the islands where they test –
Old Frenchie kills them with the Fallout
And is, to the natives, a rare pest
And has driven them all out
Of their homes. And when they protest
(The Greenpeace with scruffy beard)
The French blow them up with the rest
And never a word
Is said against them. 'Tis a crime!
But that's only the Goverment,
Which ordinary folks, like yours and mine,
Can't control – perhaps they're sent
By Almighty God to try us
And the ordinary Frenchman is not cruel.
Och! let us all be pious
And no be sic a fool!

[£10 to you, Mrs McDonald, for your very good poem.]

Mirage of tangible air, heat-rippled pollened and sweet,
rises as if seen through gently vibrated cellophane, out of

pub garden well-tended beds. Blaze of a mid-day in June;
yeastily fragrant of new bread, a buff-frothed pint of bright amber,

cool on an oak table, gleams. (Inverse of Elegy, this.)
Collared doves double-moaning alarmed rise out of the road dust –

elderly woman and teenager boy (son? grandson? a nephew?)
slam the car doors and lock up, settle in yew-shaded chairs.

Briefly the boy disappears and a short time later returns with
two drinks – a cider for him, for his companion white wine.

Suddenly, right in the middle of platitudinous natter,
drips, magnified by her specs, ooze *Oh I miss him so much!*

FINAL DEMANDS

(1988)

[Clearing the family's papers for next crowd's vacant possession:
brown leaves of letters whose dead still correspond with ourselves.]

[Chucked in the Parkray, naff juvenilia...]
P_2O_5 drip-fed from a lead pipette
fails to restore dull cotyledons
Liquinured past revivfication

[Anhydrous *lauriers.* Stubbornly unrevivable old leaves.
Drying up/not drying out.] — ⌣⌣ | — ⌣⌣ | —

Crapulous death-fright at 3 in the morning, grim fantasising...
Morphean, painless, idyllic expiry, easeful, Sabaean...
duvet and pillow-case metamorphose to sweet-smelling sered leaves,
thick-fallen under two olive boles grafted, canopied tightly,
such as the storm-wrecked Laertides, life-wracked, sunk in exhausted
snug at the end of Book V...and a phial of bland analgesics
(comforting rattle) and, fumous, a single-vintage Madeira,
buttery caramel fatty, the cobwebbed bottle of Bual
stencilled COLHEITA 1915 in white relief paint runes...

dreamingly crawls and his hands have now raked a litter together,
spacious and deep, for the leafage is lying in plentiful downfall,
lays him to rest in the midst of the leaves and piles them around him,
just as a man might cover a brand with char-blacked ashes,
guarding the seed of the fire for his tribe to use in the future,
so does he deeply immerse in the fall of past generations,
litter of leaves, not from olives, but the sepia, brittle
leaves of the letters of lost correspondents, infinite, death-frail
  (Croxley, papyrus and bond), sinks in the lines of the dead.

Clutching a chicken's furcula, festively,
[dull throb in slightly purpled first knuckle joint]
  curling the left hand little finger
    tight round the bifurcate, child-tugged fusion

[twinge of it yesterday also as you played chess with the nipper...
  premature arthritis? cramp?] wish: *may they not miss me much.*

CHAPTER THE LAST

Tethered by long ropes to iron pins spiked in the sphagnum, some half-dozen skewbald ponies had been snatching at tufts of the coarse grass sprouting between gorse and ling on the Common where a gaily-painted waggon and grey-green thick canvas beehive-shaped tent betokened the eerie presence of "Mosey" the gipsy and his little tribe.

She and Mary had become aware, as they emerged from the brake, of the sweet scent of wood-smoke. An old woman attended the fire, above which swung, from an ingenious arrangement of stout sticks, a capacious char-crusted kettle, wherefrom was effused the aromatic distillation of some savoury mess redolent of garlic and wild fowls.

Upon some nearby low gnarled May bushes, richly clotted with their dollops of new curdy blossoms, hung, or rather were pierced by the sharp thorns, items of bright-hued Romany attire, freshly laundered and arrayed thus to dry, looking like nothing so much as gaudy red, green and blue parakeets perched fluttering.

Somewhat shyly had the sisters advanced, when, looking up from her culinary preoccupations, old Dalleritha, for it was none other than she, apprehended the pair and greeted them cordially enough.

After the crone's prolix wheedling preamble, so characteristic of vulgar intercourse, Emily had explained the philanthropic nature of the sisters' visit. Greedily ogling the medicinal wine reposing in Sophia's straw basket, the beldam had inadvertently run her drooling tongue in one direction across her upper lip and then back the contrary way – a bead of saliva dependant from the corner of her toothless, corrupt maw.

'I s'll be a takin' of that there in for th'old un, lady, indeed to be a savin' of yous the trouble, see?'

But Sophia had been resolute. 'No, indeed, good Mistress, for it is no imposition on my dear sister and me, and we have ventured so far from the village that it would seem a task uncompleted were we to return home without having personally seen, and enquired the health of, old Mr Moses.'

Grudgingly then, and with many a mumbled, scarcely comprehensible complaint, had the ancient materfamilias led the way to the tent of her espoused.

At the portal, rough-hewn from a forked bough of hawthorn to make an A-shaped entrance, hung a wicker cage incarcerating a brace of Woodcocks, live, with steep foreheads, large eyes and plumage all straked like dead leaves; poor hapless creatures, destined, it was little to be doubted, for the black kettle. Hard by, upon the turf, lay an old fiddle, so refulgent in the morning sunlight that its varnished curvature gleamed like burnished amber.

When the rough sacking, which served as a door, was lifted aside, there was revealed, as on their earlier visit, the seated Gipsy Moses, enthroned like a Turkish Pasha, sucking at a pungent-smelling stained clay pipe and tracing the strange symbols with charcoal upon the same sheets of skin or coarse paper.

The old man's eyes had not strayed from his weird manuscript as the visitors entered. His poor fingers, their joints and knuckles so swollen and empurpled with the arthritis that they gave the appearance of recently dug-up beetroot tubers, laboriously formed the runes which now, more than ever, reminded Emily of some dimly recollected thing.

She had thought that the hieroglyphs were similar to those shewn her by Mr Bancroft at the Horse Shoe Inn, where some skilful mason had incorporated one of the antique 'Roony Stanes' from the derelict Priory into the steps of that hostelry's mounting-block. Like those forgotten, or not yet understood, utterances, which one could not help but contemplate as one mounted to the saddle in Bancroft's courtyard, these scripts seemed half to reveal and half conceal some strange sad mystery.

* * * *

Or was this, perhaps, the nature of all things written? With an impotent sigh, Emily crumpled the sepia-scrivened leaves, and turned abstractedly towards the hearth. At the last moment, however, she paused and considered once more the timeless, anonymous copper-plate of her dead relative. She turned from the flames and, as the dark-eyed gipsy had done so many years before, committed the dry leaves to the long box.

[Punctual, these (with a 40th birthday card) proofs are delivered –
dust-jacket mug-shot confirms eyebag-puff/jowl-blubber/flab.]

Ave!, impartial Viral Democracy
(heightening all shared vulnerability):
down-and-out/Duchess; meths bum/MP;
temp and autocratrix; Tongan/Taffy...

Chief Cop and high-ranking Sky-Pilot rail of Jovian Vengeance
(*H. sap's* unable to countenance populational thrivings
where organisms involved harm or compete with itself).

Summit of scared multinational ideological disparates
(desperate governments limply prescribe us inadequate Johnnies):
panic-created new pals join in Confederate Fright.

Feb 9/2/44
Horse Shoe Cottage
Breedon

To The Commanding Officer
Dear Sir,
J being the mother of CH/X104783 Marine Bancroft T. RM Eng Commond's am writing you regards my son J should like you to try and do me a favour if at all possible J am a widow and J live in house was my late husbands but he is gone God rest him J should like to know if my son could be released from the forces to work in the big estate farm should you find it possible to do grant me this favour you could write the Under Manager Estate Office Tonge and ask him if work is available for my son so hoping you will do your best for me J am

sir

yours faithfull

Mrs A Bancroft

Everton Boots Rule, Fazzy Fucked Paki Lou,
Quo, Fuck the Pope, Send Black Jungle Bunny Back,
Mally Cas, Beano, Fuck King Billy,
Abo-Gaz, Waterloo Skins Rule, Fu Fu.

(Thick rhododendrons and rusted rails ringed the, even then, disused
open-air bandstand-cum-theatre's crumbling dais, behind which,
stucco, a saucer-like cowl ricocheted a player's performance
– when we were in the IVth we used to trespass there in the long
hols,
strutted the platform *brief candling* it in Thespian piss-take.
Weeds sprouted from the cracked stage.

Weeds overwhelm the wrecked stage.
Urinous, fire-gutted shell in the razed park 26 years on:
pink and fluorescent blue aerosol-written runic sub-lingo...)

Cadder shag Abo-Gaz, Kiddo de Wanker, Death to all Kop Boots,
L.F.C., Booby Jill SUCKS! Chazza, Fatz Kooly, White Shit.

Trollies marked Kwik Save poke wheels and baskets from
thick-frozen slurry massed in the paddle-pool;
their wires, wind-twanged, zither. Coke cans'
light alloy clackily rolls on chimed ice,

stuttering, blown, tintinnabulant: — — | — ˘ ˘ | — —
— ˘ ˘ | — ˘ ˘ | — || [Bleakly harmonious grot.]

['Doesn't he ever write about *happiness?*' –
Husband & Wife & Daughter – A Pastoral...]

Thrill of a kite held, twine pulled gust-jerkily
with the slack, tow, taut, tug of a fishing line;
donnée of time and *propre* cartography
(sunrise in Callow Valley); peaceful
[mawkish the platitudes], joyful also...

Most savoured plump pork pie ever picnicked-on,
gleaming, the glazed baked crust, like a varnished Strad;
relish of Meaux tang, crunch-grained; brittle,
peppery, fluted columns of celery;
hot earthy radishes; crisp frilled lettuce;
bottles of Bass, beck-cold, effervescent gold,
yeasty the foam. Plush cushions of whinberry,
sheep-nibbled, silver-lichened, deep-pillow us...

Paean to celebrate this: [pastoral, cliché, old hat –
blush at the schmaltzy word] Love [but today it *is*, though, it *is* this].

Tonge, January 12th, 1857.

Dear Emily,

I am very glad to hear that you are well my dear. I wish you a very happy new-year. I have made a song for the church and it has been printed and sung at the school room at Breedon, and Mr Close requested that the children should meet at our house at Tonge on Christmas Eve in order that they might go round Tonge and Breedon to sing Christians Awake and my cards which were printed commencing "God Save our Church & State". Mr Close sent Edwin down with a meat pie of about 14 pound weight, and a Gallon of ale and two large bottles of elderberry wine. There were fifteen altogether that went round. Edwin took his fiddle and Ambrose the flutes, Will Beeton and William Adcock took their Violins. They got three and twenty shillings and sixpence. Your dear little brother Abraham stood on the dining table at Mr Bostock's and got 10d more than the rest. I have been to spend an evening with Mrs Charlton. She was very glad to see me and sent your Grandmother some apples and mince pie. I went for tea to Mrs Ashes of Breedon — Miss Ashes gave me a pretty mat, Mr Joyce gave me a new book to write poetry in, Anne gave me a beautiful drawing of her own.

Ambrose has been very poorly this week but is now rather better. Your Grandmother too has been much weaker of late, she is unaccountably pleased with your letter — she would have it in her possession and said she would have it printed. So pleased to think that you would come in May, (if all be well) to see us. Heppy Joyce came one day, but she went back the same night — she gave her best love to you. Dear Emily have you heard that Mr George Dexter of London died the week before last? I think you have not or you would have said some thing about it. My cousin John Dexter received a letter last week that he was buried on New-years day — I am exceedingly sorry as it was a great consolation for me to think that you had a relation so near at hand, for I had a very high esteem for my dear cousin George Dexter — who, I believe, was a very good man, by the grace of God, especially of late. Poor Mrs Dexter — I wish I could see her to grieve with her. Mr Bancroft at the Horse Shoe Inn, Breedon, is dead and was buried on New-years day and poor Mrs Bancroft is also very poorly. I have not seen any of Mr Bostock's family to speak to them very lately, only at church. I have taken Miss Eliza a bunch of snow-drops this new year and wished her the compliments of the Season. That is all. May God bless you my dear Emily, and grant that you may spend the next year better than you have ever spent one in your life, and that we all may is your dear Mother's wishful prayer. Little Bunting often talks and cries about your being gone, but is so very much pleased with thinking of your coming in May — I hope nothing will happen to prevent it. Send a letter as soon as convenient to let us know how you are going on and if you are well in the midst of the grime and high buildings of the Metropolis. Every one of the family sends his love, Dear Emily, and I have more poetry for you. I am glad to hear that you have prayers every night. Here is The Song.

God save our Church and State
Keep them inviolate
    'Stablished and pure,
From all false doctrines free
And Papal heresy
We as a Nation Pray
    Keep us secure.

Britons once more strike home
Tell the proud Church of Rome
    That we despise
All her idolatries
Masses and mummeries,
And pray that she may fall
    Never to rise.

Season of dangerous nincompoops daubing cul-de-sac stark walls
prettily bright tangerine: MURDER THE FUCKING SHITE POPE.

25 yards away there is a bleak brick aerosolled dead-end –
LONG LIVE THE POPE/ORANGE SHIT lividly sprayed emerald.

(Similar sentiments stimulate crazed trog footy fans' scrawlings –
LCFC KILL THE REST – baying for mashed flesh and gore.)

Mad, atavistic – REMEMBER SIXTEEN NINETY in orange;
squirted in green, SMASH THE PRODS. 12th of July, '86:

ludicrous faithfuls in camouflaged shirts and black Balaclavas
romp in each other's spilt guts; Prods, internecines, RCs...

Season and geography fecund of microcephalic idiots –
clad in absurd fancy dress, sect, in good faith, *purées* sect.

[Strike out the old { gratuitous scrivening / gratuitous lunacies / obsessional nastiness.]

Four million
~~Three hundred~~ years of intractable nitwits' blathersome humbug
[reader, conceive, if you will, a failed solicitor's plaque:

etched into verdigris *Clio & Co., incorporating*
War-Drum & Tub-Thump & Cant]
kneecapping, spatter and splat }
poesy, prattle and prate }

Royal Marine Engineer Commando,
Hightown Barracks,
Wrexham,
Denbighshire.

11th February, 1944.

Mrs. A. Bancroft,
Horse Shoe Cottage,
Breedon-on-the-Hill.

Dear Mrs Bancroft,

I regret it is not possible for me to assist in obtaining your son's release from the Forces. It has been laid down by higher authority that neither RM Tradesmen nor ranks of the Special Service Group are eligible for return to civilian occupations.

If any relaxation of these instructions occurs, I will most certainly help.

Yours,

P. Fashpoint-Shellingem

P. Fashpoint-Shellingem (Major RM).

From:
Major P. Fashpoint-Shellingem
Royal Marines.
OC RM Engineer Commando.

Squashed polystyrene Indian Take-Out trays,
eddying grease-smirched chip-papers, Pepsi cans,
scuttering plastic cups... a *Mirror's*
double-page centre-spread, caught in grained wind,

lifts on a gritty, urinous-odoured gust,

levitates, kite-like, gale-buoyed, higher,

rises in slow flaps, graceful, up-spiralling,

soars to the 19th storey, with pulchritude

slaps against, clingingly hugs

one of the uppermost panes.

Squalor Magnificat, grot, secular ecstasy Hymn,
squall-agitated filth and a high-rise worthy of Paean.]

[Grot is a great democrat. *H. sap* consanguined by waste...
cultural disparates, sub-trog and top prof, Chernobyl/Chelsea
– suddenly neighbourly now: mutual Geigered air croaks.]

Hail, democratic impartiality –
acid rain laced with lethal reactor-leak,
frozen in pills, percusses, fairly
riddles the brainpans of vassals/viscounts...

Emerald digits heralding increases
glow from the charcoaly VDU screens

nineteen floors up where populous feculence
blands, with cathartic distance, to picturesque.
Suddenly, borne on some freak updraught,
double-page-spread of a *Daily Mirror*

(EFFORTS ARE NOW BEING MADE TO ENCASE THE DAMAGED REACTOR)
presses against the bright pane,
clings, and remains, and remains

Tonge, March 7th, 1857.

My dear Emily,

I did not finish my last letter in consequence of Miss Bowman coming in, and now I bless God in all his goodness and mercy that I am able to write once more. I am like one just risen from death, and I am thinking you had better have a mother with but one breast than to have no mother at all — I know the loss of the best of Mothers.

The country about here has been all on a move respecting me and I cannot think the Queen herself would have had so much real kindness shewn to her. We have visitors every day, and at the first more than we could do with — every one seemed to think it their duty to bring me a present, so that, set it in what light you may, there is infinite mercy attending it. So, I must tell you the wound is healing nicely, but, you may be sure it will not feel as usual — it has grown up partly, and I am thankful the dangerous tumour is removed.

Miss Eliza Bostock attends to me well and has given me a very nice new cloth jacket lined with purple silk and trim'd with beautiful silk braid — she has also given me a dozen of fine Stout from Cox & Malin, a hamper almost as much as a man could carry. Mrs Bostock comes and brings me pots of nice lemon jelly, quart pots — she sent little Joey with 14 new laid eggs and a bottle of Sherry, also broth with Sherry in it and yesterday they sent the Girl with a bird nicely cooked and plenty of gravy. Mrs Curzon *sent me Bla-mange and nice mould puddings, Mr J. Bulstrode and Mrs Cross a bottle of good old Sherry, Miss Pegg of Colk a beautiful fowl and eggs, Mr Joyce a fowl, Mrs Joyce a brace of Partridges, Miss Bancroft brought me a basketful of new laid eggs and a large pot of Raspberry-jam, Miss Tompson of our town two bottles of coltsfoot wine, Mr John Joyce a plumb cake, Mrs Mugglestone a large plate of roast veal, Wm. Charlton 2 pots of jam, Lewis a bottle of elder wine, Bessy a bottle of Port, Mrs Eagelfield a part of nice pheasant, Miss Cowlishaw a plate of roast hare & currant jelly, next day light pudding garnished with apricot cheese, Tom a doz Oranges, Thompsons a lot of apples, Fanny a lot of figs, Mr Joyce a bottle of old Port wine, also Mr William half a pint of Brandy, Mr Allan a quart of Port wine, Mr Dawker a fine Woodcock in the feathers all bar'd & bestrak'd as dead leaves of Autumn. But you know there must be such things or I could not have survived the loss of blood and the anguish, and we have been obliged to have folks work here and your Aunts must not want whilst they are sat up with me and attending on me. Sophia had a bed in the corner of the room, while I was extremely bad, but now she sleeps with me again. We have had a leg of mutton or beef every week since I came up stairs — which will soon be 8 weeks. We have had plenty of coal during my illness and the fire up stairs has never been out — we have burnt a cart load, and John sent me some more yesterday. None can behave better to me than they do, God bless them. Write directly.*

Yr Loving Mother

[Alcaic (rendered Lounge Bar colloquial):]
Myrsilus dead! Get pissed at the joyous news!…

{ formally elegant
[(Turbulent content { metrically dignified.)
Mad despot captains *still* scuttle ships of state –
cudgel-thud, steel-clank, shell-zap, gas-sough,
feculent bilge of the urban { frontline…]
{ scuppers

Futile pathetic kindly-meant circular:
'We are inviting patients about your age…
please bring along a urine sample…
blood pressure tendency… at Health Centre…'

[*What's 40 years here or there on the chrono-stratigraph?*, you wrote.
Striking a stance, you were, then; really believe it, though, now.]

[Mostly it's other people's death sentences
one has adopted, striking an attitude;
suddenly, though…] Among a mess of
skeleton, puckered skin, part-consumed flesh,

I tug a bifurcate bone with my daughter, win, and, in secret,
wish *When I rattle my clack, may she not too deeply grieve.*

Lodge Gate House,
Ashbourne Park,
Thorpe.

Dec 21. 44

The C.O. Sir — Is it possible for me to have my son released from the service on compassionate grounds? I am a widow now also I have bad health — periods of arthritis when I need someone in the home to help me. This prevents me from taking a situation. I have only my 10/- pension and a small allotment from my sons pay each week. He is Po.X. 101922 (T) Mne (L/Cpl) B. Hurt Royal Marine Eng: Commando. He has taken part in the D. Day assult also the French Coast many times and to Holland — he now suffers with Sciatica and in my humble opinion this renders him unfit for the Commando work. I need him very much here.

Yours Faithfully

Mrs J. Hurt.

[Three-day abdominal pain: dead scared – the liver/the plonk?
Sudden recovery; with renewed vigour, vivid perception…]

Freezing fog – shivering rooks huddle, wings grizzled with frost.
Lipstick-smudged fag-end, still fulminant, fizzes steam on a wet grave.

Loud from a garage a PFSST sternutates in the air-hose.
Bickering Pepsi tins emptily clack on ice-skinned canal top.

Out of an overflow pipe, ice drools, off-white congealed wax.
[Ossless, quotidian; worth, through revived awareness, a paean.]

Under a clay weight dumped on the leather-topped
desk in his study, final demands, accrued
    quarterly/monthly (Access, phone bill,
        water rates, overdraft, life insurance),

flutter in rose-fumed draughts from the garden. [40th birthday…
    chequebook – the Mrs and kid shan't, at least, be bequeathed debt.]

Lodge Gate House,
Ashbourne Park,
Thorpe.

Jan 1. 45

Sir — A short time ago I wrote you requesting the release of my son from the service. I now realise how very mistaken I was in doing this and of perhaps giving you the impression that he had failed to help me. I assure you sir that this is not so, and that every week I have had adequite assistance from him. He was unaware that I thought of applying for his release. He is one of the very best and I feel ashamed that I may have damaged his reputation in your eyes. We both realise the importance of everyone doing and giving their upmost in the next few months. My only excuse is that I have just lost my husband and at the time of writing you last I was feeling the loss and loneliness and did not consider the consequences to my son as I should. He is one of the bravest and best so will you forget that I ever asked for his release

Yours Faithfully
Mrs J. Hurt.

Flushed from meshed rust and ginger dead bracken and
bramble, a woodcock, russet-barred, uncalling,
    swishes, explodes up, plumply zigzags.
        Underfoot: oval of steaming cupped stalks

faintly imprinted in frost-silvered leaf-mould, fecal sac still warm,
    chestnut-edged buff wisp of down, { instants of tangible loss
                                                                    { instance

frail wisps bestraked like dead leaves

August 11th 1857

My dear Daughter,

I feel rather better this morning and am at Ashbourne Park. You may be sure I am wondering what you are all about this morning and what they are doing at Tonge without me. I am afraid the constant rain will injure the crops that are almost ripe for cutting. I have been writing a few lines —

The Trees in Ashbourne Park are Green
The Flowers are really Glowing —
But nothing like our own Sweet Rill
Forever ever flowing.

Thorpe Cloud may frown upon the Dove
Down at his foot low gliding
But Tonge's the Valley that I love
The place I would abide in.

None so sweet as the Valley of my own dear [foxing and the fold of the paper render this paragraph illegible]

I wrote one half of this letter a day or two ago, but first one wants me & then another so I divide my time as well as I can amongst them all, and I am sorry to say Bessy Hurt is in a very poor way just now. She is 7 months gone in pregnancy, and often obliged to be in bed. It was her birthday on Sunday but she was forc'd to take her dinner in bed. We were all in Hurt's great room — we had a leg of Mutton & Caper sauce, a laid pudding & jellies and Plumb Cake at Tea, wine and biscuits after. I am glad to say she is rather better today. I am expecting to leave here every day now — so I shall call to stay at Derby if I am not sent for home. Write a little line to me my love. I feel nervous about them at home. Excuse me this time — I will write again soon — with love to dear John, I remain, my best beloved child,

Yr affectionate Mother.

{ topography
Donnée of time and { cartography – *Ashes Valley at sunset*:
duck-egg gashed gold, splashed maroon; dulling to indigo bruise.

1859 Plan of the Camberwell Cemetery, Forest Hill Road, S.E. Published by H. Cornford, Monumental Sculptor, Adjoining Entrance, Forest Hill Road, Peckham Rye. (Memorials of every description Restored and Renovated. Inscriptions Engraved. Imperishable Letters in Stone, Marble, or Granite. 30 Years Established. Illustrated Designs upon Application, or Free By Post. Special Fancies will be prepared when required.)

On verso, tremulous sepia holograph: Grave this, ornate, in Granitt – *'In Loving Memry of Thomas Ashbourne Hurt, Infant Son of Thomas and Elizabeth Hurt, Died March 11th, 1859, Aged 17 Months.'*

10 years and 3 months old; on the paper-white
temple, a turquoise vein like a hieroglyph;
Lucozade, crumbs of cake – each bird-sip
after a minute is puked up, rancid;

flaxen hair shed in handfuls, her cranium
bald as a pawn (unkind chemotherapy).
Medic and poetaster glibly
(equally impotent platituders)

tender inadequate barbs.

Yesterday's lorry's blackstrap delivery –
(26 tonnes) the tanker bloke couldn't quite
get it all in; the pipes, uncoupled,
leaked a few gallons of glossy, thick gunge.

So, in the alley by the molasses tank,
next to the wheat and maize-gluten intake pit,
viscid morass of inch-deep treacle,
under a skin of chaff, oozes, sticky.

Recently fledged, three *Passer domesticus*,
lured by the grained crust, flounder in gluey drool,
primaries syruped, eyes sealed sweetly,
flap, flop amorphously, blackstrapped dumplings.

Three-fingered Fazzy, hard-case, the Grinderman,
gathers them gently into his denim bib,
nestles them fondly, runs warm water
into the millworkers' bog's cracked wash-bowl,

mumblingly croons as he cleanses the sweet down *Frail little poor things*
[*poor little frail little things; frail little poor little things*].

On the same front page: **ARABS IN A-BOMB BID/**
NHS BOSS BACKS HIV VIRUS BLITZ.
From the Globe's fag-smoked beery parlour:
...course it's the kiddies as I feels for like,

see worra means like, they Middle Easter lot,
them gets the hay bomb, that's like the hultimate,
once them starts lobbin they fings round mate
no fuckergonnerav no chance mister,

them's got this Hallah (that's like the gord theym got),
them reckons all folks should ave this Hallah chap,
that's why them ates they Jooz an that see,
they Middle Easters'll start the Fird War,

same as they Haids as theym got in the *Sun* like, trouble o Haids is...
[Poor kids, twice-vulnerable: some other godly twits' war/

your own too-dangerous love.]

Tonge, March 12th, 1859.

My dear Emily,

It is my very painful task to tell you that your beloved sister Sophia Mary expired at 3 this morning after a very severe conflict with her last enemy Death — but she has done with all her sufferings now and entered on Glory everlasting. I am distressed beyond measure that it seems you are not in a fit state to come it has pleased the Almighty to take from us the best of Daughters and most caring of all sisters — cannot tell you what I passed through tell you how very distressed I am to let you know but if I did not I should be very uneasy I do not know what I am doing by letting you know — use all the fortitude you can and she is Happy and all is well — ah! frail poor little frail beings — Oh I have much to tell you — tell John she would be pleased I am sure if he could come and attend her remains to the Grave.

Emily I do not know how I write I have written to most of her cousins this morning God be with us I want some one to hold my distressed trembling heart this is the greatest sorrow I have ever felt — pray — pray for me — your Aunt is here and I have Jane Bonson but Oh! I have not my delight my Sophy Mary my Jesus has taken my beautiful blossom at 4 and twenty Oh my Saviour keep me in the hollow of thine hand "I was not at rest, neither was I in safety neither was I quiet yet trouble came" Oh let us prepare for our last moments — that and none other is the greatest wisdom

I will not attempt to tell you my feelings for it is in vain

Come or send but you very like cannot come, as from the nature of your dear sister's disease she cannot be kept long I cannot act I am so very shattered with musing and extream sorrow & grief, write to me and I will answer it immediately Yr Loving much distressed Mother.

Thirty years friendship, brief letters latterly,
mostly on matters ornithological,
so it's an automatic mental
tic to compose as I do this evening

Very good views of Buteo lagopus,
dark carpal patches, dark tips to primaries,
terminal broad dark band to white tail –
do you remember that one we saw in...?

then to recall that to do so is nuts. To you Marie, therefore,
(since it's pathetic and mad to address oneself to the dead)

I re-address these notes on the raptor [even though, really,
it's not yourself but your son with whom I still correspond].

Thick rhododendrons curtained the, even then,
mouldering disused outside proscenium,
crumbling dais backed by a stuccoed cowl
from which a player's lines would be ricocheted
into the bosky shades of a city park's
shrubby, neglected corner. A Lower IVth
strutted the wormed boards cockily *Out, out*ing,
callowly slighting time and Melpomene.

Urinous, burnt-out, relic of civic wealth
29 years on: wintery sun projects
(onto flaked stucco daubed with despair-runes) a
palimpsest walking shadow. A fingernail
rot-tests the wreckage, strays to a middle-aged
wattle of jowl-flab, substance of candle-wax.

Tonge, May 19th 1861.

My Dear,

I have been writing a few lines on poor Gipsy Moses. Will you accept them?

Ye little birds on every bough
Hush! while that dark eye closes
While the mist of death hangs on the brow
Of sprightly Gipsy Moses.

Ye winds a solemn silence keep
Stir not the wild hedge roses
Disturb ye not the last frail sleep
Of dark-ey'd Gipsy Moses.

As some fair flower on Beauty's wreath
Droops ere the sun light closes
So look'd he on his bed of death
The lovely Gipsy Moses.

And Ah! his favourite violin
Apollo thou shalt take it
For it would a be cruel sin
For mortal hand to wake it,

And rather to the Ocean's brine
Poor Mosey I would toss it
Than any other hand than thine
Should draw the bow across it.

The dust lies on his coffin lid
On him the green sward closes
But fairer flower earth never hid
Than dark-ey'd Gipsy Moses.

Poor Moses is buried at Witwake near the Charnwood Forest. Old Dalleritha has been ill ever since he died. You remember your dear sister Sophy Mary sending him the arrow root and wine? — she would not let Dalleritha take it in fear she should drink it herself — you remember taking it to the tent [foxed and faded beyond comprehensibility] *for we bring our years to an end like a tale that is told. Yr Loving Mother.*

Knobbled amorphous purple grotesqueries,
tubers of malformed beetroot – the *saucisson*
  arthritic fingers of my father
    fumblingly clutch at a worn-smooth pawn skull,

counter, at least for a couple of moves, the pressing advance of
  (tongue-lolling, wild-eyed) the crazed palfrey of pale polished ash.

[Clearing the family's home for the next crowd's vacant possession:
  long box of letters whose dead scribes correspond with us still.]

Tonge, July 21st, 1862

It gives me joy in the midst of all my sorrows to know that you have made up your mind to come once more through much fatigue and anxiety to see your poor dear solitary Mother, a Mother that has been longing to see you for years — day and night sighing on account of your long absence, but thank God you have made up your mind to come to your dear old Home once more. God bless you, and bring you and your babies safe to me. I am but very poorly this morning. I am at Breedon & I have enquired about what John Roulstone will charge from Ashby for 3 of you — he will charge sixpence for you and threepence apiece for the children, and I think nothing at all for the Box if it is not very large, but never mind about that for you are sure to be met with some of us. Now remember, he will start from Edmond Leawood's at the Waggon & Horses in Church Street exactly at 5-o'clock in the afternoon — but you will be met, so do not make yourself in any way uneasy about that.

Give dear Heppy Joyce's love to her dear Brother Harry, and she is in full expectation of seeing you soon now. So write again and let me know if you shall come on next Saturday or the Saturday after. Be sure you tell me exactly that there may be no mistake. I am sure there are no complaints or fevers prevalent at this time, for which I am very thankful. Do not think of bringing much luggage as you will have enough to do to bring yourselves — and the worst dresses the dears have are better than Edwin's poor children have. I want nothing in this world but to see you and the dears — I hope you will give your heart to God, for without Him we can do nothing. Pray that he will take us all under the Shadow of his wings, there is no real safety elsewhere.

Give my love to John Shoebridge and thank him for letting you come. I should indeed be most happy to see him again down in Leicestershire — I hope he will come whilst I live to see him once more. Guide us Oh! Thou great Jehovah, we are weak and frail things but Thou art Mighty. Write directly on receipt of this — I hope you will soon behold old Breedon Church, and believe me your ever dear and affectionate Mother.

[...when they read this, it may be already done...]
Low over dim pines, dactylic phrases croak
(*Scolopax rusticola* roding),
finishing off in a sneeze-like high 'tswick',

[... supine in bracken...] the only other sound is a rattle
(barbs in a brown plastic phial): — ˘˘ | — ˘˘ | —

_S_E_C_R_E_T

SUPPLEMENTARY REPORT.

On the 1st. of March, 1945, Troop H.Q. and No. 2 Section accompanied Brigade H.Q., 45 (RM) Commando and No. 6 Commando on the Advance from AFFERDEN to WELL.

The main task allocated to the Troop was the opening of the rd from AFFERDEN (M/R: 395388, Eastern Holland 1/25,000 Sheet 4302) to BERGEN Cross-Roads (M/R: 831353, Eastern Holland 1/25,000 Sheet 4302). This rd had been extensively mined, cratered and blocked. For this Operation the Section were under Command 241 Fd Company. One D.6 Bulldozer and one D.4 Bulldozer were made available to the Section. This equipment proved of great value.

The rd was of good macadam construction and visual search formines was possible. Clearance Parties checked the verges of the rd. Two other parties were employed in filling two large craters. These were filled by knocking down bombed houses with a Bulldozer and transporting the rubble to the craters by lorry and filling in. Subsequently the Bulldozers were used to remove such trees as could not be removed by hand from the rd. The enemy having retreated rapidly, the Section were able to make speedy progress and the BERGEN Cross-Roads were reccied at approximately 1500 hours.

Two large sized craters were found at this point surrounded by a barbed wire fence with "MINEN" Signs attached. A suitable: divergence existed and it was decided that it would be quicker to sweep the divergence, which consisted of a rd surface, than the crater itself. Two parties were employed on this clearance and Schumines were discovered and lifted on the verge. During this operation some type of Booby Trap was initiated by the right hand clearance party resulting in the death of CH/X104783 Marine T BANCROFT and Po.X. 101922 (T) Mne (L/Cpl) B. HURT; Po.X. 116223 Marine W.G. PALMER being severely wounded. Marine T. BANCROFT was thrown some 30 feet from the site of the explosion into the crater in the middle of the rd; L/Cpl B. HURT was thrown some 60ft into an orchard adjoining the rd; Mne W.G. PALMER was heard to cry for help and a party proceeded to probe their way towards him. When they had reached the foot of the embankment Lieut. J.J.A. MCLAREN appeared on the scene in his Jeep and proceeded to follow along the White Tape carrying First Aid equipment. When Captain P.W.J. NEALE was within a few feet of W.G. PALMER an explosion occurred which had been caused by Lieut. J.J.A. MCLAREN treading upon a Schumine. The clearing party were thrown in various directions and minor injuries caused to Capt A.B. JACKSON RM and Marine G. DOWNING. Lieut J.J.A. MCLAREN was very severely wounded in the legs. Capt P.W.J. NEALE RM then directed further clearance of Schumines to enable Lieut J.J.A. MCLAREN and Marine W.G. PALMER to be removed from the Minefield. Marine L.J. PRICE who had been following the party laying the Tape behaved with exemplary coolness despite the fact that he had been in close proximity to both explosions and had suffered a cut in the face. The casualties were successfully removed from the Minefield and evacuated immediately by ambulance. The bodies of Marine T. BANCROFT and L/Cpl B. HURT were recovered by TSM D.J.R. MORSS RM and members of the Section and burial effected on the site; it was impossible to recover any documents.

A detailed report of this incident has been rendered to the Brigade Commander.

During the night Troop supplied Mine Clearance Party under Command Cpl J. MCCORKINDALE to 45 (RM) Commando who reccied a Route from BERGEN Cross-Roads to WELL. The remainder of the Section continued to maintain the AFFERDEN-BERGEN Cross Rds road and improve the causways made over the craters.

A Bailey Bridge at AFFERDEN was also maintained by the Section.

P. Fashpoint-Shellingem (Major RM)
O.C. No.1 Troop, R.M. Engineer Commando.

Att HQ 1 Cdo Bde,
B.L.A.
5 Mar, 45.
PFS/FPC

But the *availability* of the things…
pox on all quacks who won't prescribe knock-out drops
(not with an irresponsible randomness,
but with humane good grace to ~~those~~ glum us
us
terminals knowingly ready for it).

Fleet St conveys guerrilla activity
deep in Sri Lankan forest – a cyanide
pellet depends from each one's necklace:
in the event of capture or overthrow…
infinite luxury (7 seconds).

Briefly this *gravitas* weighting the conversation at breakfast
lightens 'Gorillas, though, Dad, surely aren't clever enough?'

rustle of old gratuitous scrivenings

frail wisps of dead bestraked leaves

crackle of anhydrous bay

— ˘ ˘ | — ˘ ˘ | —
Croxley pa pyrus and bond

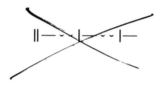

|| — ˘ ˘ | — ˘ ˘ | —

~~|| — ˘ ˘ | — ˘ ˘ | —~~

PERDUTA GENTE

(1989)

South Bank: Sibelius 5's
incontrovertible end –
five exhalations, bray of expiry,
absolute silence...

Under the Festival Hall is a foetid
tenebrous concert
strobed by blue ambulance light.
PVC/newspapers/rags
insulate ranks of expendables, eyesores,
winos, unworthies,
one of which (stiff in its cardboard Electrolux
box stencilled **FRAGILE,**
STOW THIS WAY UP, USE NO HOOKS)
officers lug to the tumbril,
exhaling, like ostlers, its scents:

squit,

honk,

piss,

meths,

distress.

London's most exciting apartments all have river views, £330,000 to £865,000

"Large homes standing in two or three acres are now selling for well in excess of £200,000," Mr Williams said.

"That means there is no shortage of people willing to pay a relatively high price for old barns so they can do them up. At the end of the day, they will have a substantial home set in several acres worth a good deal more than £200,000."

Derelict barns in south Shropshire are fetching six figure prices — and estate agents say there are no shortage of interested buyers.

A ruin at Eastham, near Tenbury, with no roof and hardly any walls is on offer for £100,000.

And an L-shaped barn with an acre of land near Worfield saw some fierce bidding between two developers before finally going under the hammer for £222,000.

Money is no object to buyers seeking a quiet country life.

A large barn at Cleobury Mortimer occupying a commanding position at the end of a mile long track has just sold for £90,000.

Another site at nearby Milson, involving the conversion of three barns standing on an acre of land, sold at £167,000.

do s s

Talk Terms Today

OR REGRET IT FOR THE REST OF YOUR LIFE

JUSTHOME

Thank You

One day a lone hag gippo arrived and
camped on the waste ground
which we traversed on our way to the school bus
every morning.

Cumulus breath puffs rose from a pink-nosed
rope-tethered skewbald.
Winter: a frost fern fronded the iced glass
caravan window
through which I ventured a peep, but I leapt back
horribly startled
when the rime cleared and an eye
glared through the hole at my own.
(Filthy she was, matted hair, withered leg and
stank of excreta.)

After that, each time we passed it we'd lob a
rock at the window.
When it was smashed she replaced it with cardboard;
one of us lit it –
she hobbled round with a pisspot and doused the
flames with its contents.
Then she gave up and just left it a gaping
black fenestration
through which we chucked bits of scrap,
rubbish, a dog turd, a brick.

But when she skedaddled, a stain,
delineating where she'd been,
etiolated and crushed,
blighted that place, and remained.

Now we arrive at the front of the ruin;
here are there moanings,
shrieks, lamentations and dole,
here is there naught that illumes.
Mucky Preece lives in a pigsty beside the
derelict L Barn,
tetrous, pediculous, skint,
swilling rough cider and Blue.
Now lie we sullenly here in the black mire –
this hymn they gurgle,
being unable to speak.
Here they blaspheme Divine Power.
Money no object to buyer of L-shaped
picturesque old barn
seeking the quiet country life
(two hundred and twenty-two grand,
Property Pages last night –
with which Mucky Preece is involved,
scraping the squit from his arse).

terribly sick with her meths, but
she kept on and on vomiting through
the night, but with nothing left to
sick up (the front of her scraggy
overcoat covered in the methsy,
vegetable-soupy slime — the
stench abominable) so that
between honks she screamed hor-
ribly. The only sleep we got was
after one of the old hands dragged
her off, still screaming, and dumped
her in the alley round the corner
where the dustbins are.
Today is Monday: in St. Botolph's
crypt they give out free clothes to us

missiz an me inda warm inda Euston
        unnerground buskin
fugginwell busted armonica playin
        only da one fing
    over an zover again

missiz gone arse-over-ed on da fuggin
        down eshcalator
tryin to swing for some cuntinna bowler
        wot givver two pee
    bazshd up er face an er arm
    cetched up er sleeve in da fing
    where it gozsh clackety-clack
    mergency stop button presh

mashessa blood inna cetchup da coppers
        draggin er screamin
still wiv er good arm out of er pocket
        bockle uv Strongbow

gizzera fifty or twenny fer fuggsay
        mister a tellya
    savvy dis noosepaper see?
    sonly bed we gotter nigh

Remedy

Now that the hanging of murderers has been rejected by Parliament (myself I look upon hanging as barbaric) there is a simple alternative which will give the

They give them too much money to hang about the streets and not to look for work.

They should stop the dole money or cut it in half.

It would stop them

That remedy is to chop off his right leg and his left arm. After all, to give a prisoner a life sentence, he could be out in about 16 years.

EX-SOLDIER
(Name and address supplied)

EX-SOLDIER
(Name and address supplied)

— chop both his arms off. He couldn't do much with his feet.

We come to the person who goes to the dole office and states, by putting his signature to a piece of paper, that he is not working, that done, he then jumps into his car to do a 60 hour week.

The hand that puts his signature to paper should also be chopped off.

Some say they will fight on the beaches. It is a pity they weren't fighting during the war, a bit of army service would do them good.

Cut dole

cut

Gente perduta, wino-unworthies,
knackered-up dipsos,
swilling *rosato*-and-meths –
we snooped a look in their lairs

while they were beachcombing: still-viscid meths-puke,
faeces, a mattress,
cardboard, an old plywood door,
wedged in the clefts of the dunes.

Sweet from the pines wafts a resinous fragrance
pungent with sea smells
(molluscs, salinity, kelp);
regular clank of a bell

tolls from a wreck-buoy, swung by the reflux;
wardens in green jeeps,
dapperly-uniformed, plump
skedaddlers of squatters and tramps,

patrol what aspires to **Reserve of Endangered
Natural Habitats;**
a yellow and black JCB
scrunches shacks into a skip.

author's last review which speaks of 'post-Chernobyl reindeer piled in a ruck in the tundra... trains with their burden of sinister finned flasks [rumbling] ominously on and on through a benighted city where trash amasses, the loonies and dispos [*sic* (presumably dispossessed)] proliferate and the resident strumpet of the Globe opines "If you ask me, this planet is fucked; not just me, love, the whole planet, fucked".' This, scribbled as circumstances permitted, between the derry (derelict house) and St Botolph's crypt where the destitute alcos

102

today. I got some trousers but they had very bad stains down the front and the knees were both in tatters and they stank. The woman in front of me got a yellow vest but said she could see lice and fleas in it and called the vicar a fucking cunt.

Tuesday: In the crypt of St. Botolph's we got a mug of tea and some bits of bread. It's like a sort of air-raid shelter with us all waiting for something awful to go away, or, worse, to happen.

Friday 19th: got some Strongbow with this old shitty dosser, bloke

Snarl of a JCB, cordon of Old Bill,
    megaphone rasping
  into a 3 a.m. squat.

Sleep-fuddled dissolutes, still dressing cold dis-
    consolate bratlings,
  struggle with carrier-bags.

One of the Council Bailiffs is sporting a
    Have a Nice Day badge
  fixed on the yellow hard hat.

Often at dusk in the birch woods beyond the
gates of the city,
you see the glimmer of fires of the hapless
dispossessed losers.

One of these, russetly lit from beneath by
fulminant embers,
howls through the tenebrous gloom –
something concerning smoked fish,
black bread and vodka, I think.

Distant, a plangently-played balalaika ac-
companies wailing
vocals whose burden is loss –
Gone are the youthfully beautiful whom I
loved in my nonage;
strength and vitality, gone;
roof-tree and cooking-hearth, gone.

Eyes like an elephant's, blood-bleared and tiny,
gowkily ogle;
tremulous wart-knuckled pachyderm fingers
fumble a tin cup;
skewers of carp flesh fumed to mahogany;
dark-crusted rye loaf;
sloshed spirit hissing in ash.

103

who, like me, is no stranger to the pig-pen o' nights, told me how he went to the Spike last night, but was so rough still from the surgical spirit that he fell down the stone stairs and smashed his face up badly. They told him to fuck off and come back when he was better. He did a Skipper last night on the kitchen window-ledge of the Royal Hotel – you get a bit of warmth through the glass – but the police came round and moved him on. Tues 23rd.: The same bloke I was on about yesterday got given a quid, so we got this tin of Carlsberg Sp

Don't think it couldn't be you –
bankrupted, batty, bereft,
huddle of papers and rags in a cardboard
spin-drier carton,
bottle-bank cocktails and Snow soporifics,
meths analgesics,
beg-bucket rattler, no-hope no-homer,
squatter in rat-pits,
busker in underground bogs
(plangent the harp-twang, the *Hwaet!*
Haggard, the youthful and handsome whom I
loved in my nonage;
vanished, the vigour I valued;
roof-tree and cooking-hearth, sacked).
Bankrupted, batty, bereft-
don't think it couldn't be you.

gizzera quiddora fiftyfer fuggsay
        mistera tellya
tellya da missiziz fugginwell whatnot
        fugginwell ampute
    afer da nackerup arm

armazzerfuggerup der inda Euston
        afera go down
    arse-over-ed in da fing
    waz ish osh clackeshy-clig

missiziz gointer ospical ad da
        whassizname tashun

    tashun da arm as iz skwozsh
    cuts ov da armaziz skwozsh
    nowizza bagwiv one arm
    ospical calls amputaysh

109

and have been not infrequently covered in the crusted slurry of the base beasts with whom I had shared a night's accommodation.

At about this time yesterday, the St. Mungo's crowd came round on the soup run. Nuns called the Poor Sisters of the Mother of God, or some such crap, dishing us all out with plastic cups of thin brown broth and a couple of slices of dry white Mother's Pride. One of the blokes under the fly-over climbed into the van and got his dick out. He's a Brasso addict and was sick all over the chief nun and

That one is Boris the Swine
(known as 'the Swine' for the fact that he sometimes
falls in the swine-pen
when he is terribly drunk –
covered in slurry for days),
but we must make allowances, since he
worked at the Station
when the – remember the headline
**(Efforts are now being made to encase the
damaged reactor)**?

Often at evening he plangently strums and
bays from the birch wood,
where he reposes, this strain:
Nothing can ever be done;
things are intractably thus;
all know the bite of grief, all will be brought to
destiny's issue;
those who have precognition suffer
sorrow beforehand;
bodies are bankrupt, the main Expedition has
left us behind it.

Probable Effects o

RADIATION PROTEC-
TION PROCEDURES

system unit

Acute Exposure
(Gamma Rads)

Widespread experimental work with m
has confirmed the volatile nature of fission p
fault conditions. This was discussed more ful
concluded that for the purpose of overall asse
assume that the gaseous and volatile fission p
tions relative to one and other in which they
xenon, iodine, tellurium, caesium and rutheniu
fission products of importance. From the expe
not appear to be volatile in the conditions of
reasonable accord with the evidence and a reas
to take the release of strontium isotopes, exp
activities of the isotopes present in fuel, as
assumed for the release of gaseous and volatil
activities of important fission products prese
fuel are given in Table II of Lecture No. 6.

DISPERSION OF RADIOACTIVITY IN THE ATMOSPHERE

3. Pasquill's method of calculating the
in the atmosphere is in use in the U.K.[1]. I
known theoretical treatment by Sutton[2] to gr
empirical correlation of measurements made to

Mortality of employees
Energy Authority,

January, 2 a.m.:
at roost on the window-ledge outside a hotel's
kitchen a dirty
hirsute in three overcoats
snuggles against frosted glass where a cabbage-
smelling Vent-Axia
sussurates vestigial warmth.

Muezzins were Tannoying dirgefully from the
        mosques in the fountained
squares of the Turkish end of the city;
        barbecued goats' smoke
    swealed from ramshackle cafés.

Stallholders (leather and pewterware) tweaked the
        sleeves of the wealthy
Euro/American/Japanese gawpers
        thronging the cramped wynds;
    fezzed coffee-drinkers played chess.

Squatting in alley-muck, whining, a woman
        cradled a frail child;
two other infants with counterfeit blindness,
        rattling beg-bowls,
    obediently foamed at the mouth –

manifest mendicant mountebanks (though their
        glee was authentic
    when you disburdened yourself
    of that frayed ten-dinar note).

Worse than the Shakes is the Horrors – the rats and
echoing voices...

echoing voices
under the flyover, rubble and streets of
boarded-up derries –
No Go for ambulance, fire-brigade, milkman,
Post Office, Old Bill...

when they demolished his sty
Mucky Preece, alias Tucker,
tramped from the sticks to the Borough –
his mother was only a gippo,
his only possession a bucket...

sometimes it seems like a terrible dream, in
which we are crouching
gagged, disregarded, unsought
in dosshouses, derries and spikes,
and from which we shall awake,

mostly it seems, though, we won't.

ernobyl ac

Unit 4 of the Cher-
c Soviet Union is the
has ever occurred at a
lant, in several respects:
f human casualties, in the
released, in the
t, and in the
-strained
too

14 speech on the
tion confirmed th
week earlier by a
the International
that the initiating
excursion within t
At the time of th
was at a power le
or 200 MWt. Since
the first two victin
adjustor of a
nerator of
ms l

Some workers must have got their skin
contaminated while removing their out
the vault. Improper handling of comm
contamination. From there, the contan
areas around Unit 1 including the Retu
other workers.

Radioactive contamination in the air

a. Particulate (or dust)

b. Vapour - Iodine, $1H^3$

c. Gaseous - Argon-41, Xe-135, Kr-88

Particulate activity is measured by co
a high efficiency filter and counting
Continuous monitors are of two types.

could have expected that the author himself would have plumbed such depths of filth, depravity and degradation. For, indeed by his own account (the MS Diaries, pp.101-113), he was by this time: 'no stranger to the pig-pen o'nights'; 'not infrequently covered in the crusted slurry of the base beasts with whom [*sic*] [he] had shared a night's accommodation'; 'acquainted with the subtleties of the Bottle-Bank Cocktail, the urinous scent of the squat, the needle's brief oblivion, grief's bite'.

And then, to the indescribable squalor of

Under the concreted cantilevered
haven of arty
spans of the *Bibliothek*,
shivering dossers each evening repose in
newspaper bivvies.
Mornings, they head for the park.

Slats of the frost-crusted park benches steam in
8 a.m. sunlight.
Scavenging corvine-clawed men
rifle each *Abfalleimer*, greedily
glean after rye crusts
flung for gross ducks near the lake,

swig the sour dregs of the bottle-bank empties,
Tafelwein, Schaumwein,
Spätlese, Steinhäger, Schnapps.
Today I have planted a two-kilo *Schinken*
where they will find it
[hooray for the secular saint].

Course ee woz always the Black Sheik of the
        family, ee woz,
    went to une versity too
    (done moths an physicals there),

ad a good job ee did too with that Anat-
        omical Engy,
    then ee dripped out on the dole,
    got on the booze an them dregs

(cococo whatsisname, you know, the white stuff),
        now ees a squitter,
    lives in a squit with no rent,
    eed ad a radio dose.

How doeth the citie sit solitarie that
was full of people?
She that was great among nations hath no
comforter, all her
friends haue dealt treacherously.

Something is in the air, more and more nutters,
alcos and dossers,
dole diuturnal.

Sometimes it seems like a terrible dream from
which we'll awaken;
but mostly it seems that we won't.

Let us descend, though, through urinous subways to
miseries greater,
al doloroso ospizio, where the
newly tormented
sample new torments.

Woe vnto them that decree
vnrighteous decrees and that turn
the needy from iustice and robbe
the rights from the poore of my people.

What will ye doe with yr wealth
in the day of the storme which shall come
from afarre, when all that remaines
is to crouch with those ye haue oppressed?

te Whole Body Doses

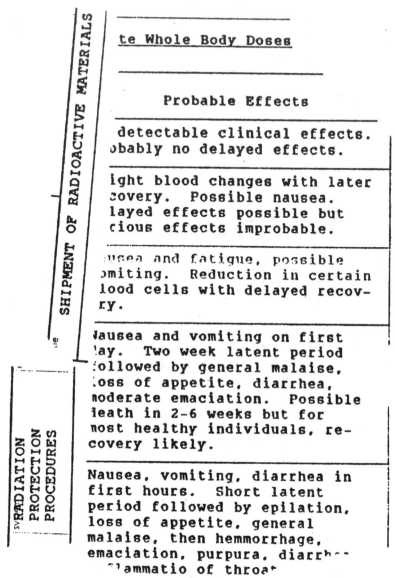

Probable Effects
detectable clinical effects. obably no delayed effects.
ight blood changes with later covery. Possible nausea. layed effects possible but rious effects improbable.
usea and fatigue, possible omiting. Reduction in certain lood cells with delayed recovery.
Nausea and vomiting on first lay. Two week latent period followed by general malaise, loss of appetite, diarrhea, moderate emaciation. Possible death in 2-6 weeks but for most healthy individuals, recovery likely.
Nausea, vomiting, diarrhea in first hours. Short latent period followed by epilation, loss of appetite, general malaise, then hemmorrhage, emaciation, purpura, diarrh-- -lammatio of throat first

Most of them quietly left when the Council
put in the Bailiffs
(3 in the morning it was);
but one nutter stayed there holed up,

stuck his head out of the fourth-storey smashed-paned
window and hollered
Don't think it couldn't be you.
Then he began chucking rats –

ten or a dozen big dead ones (the squat was
full of them, we found,
when we moved in with the dozers).
Queerest thing of the lot

was he came to the window and empted a briefcase
full of these *papers*,
hundreds of fluttering sheets
caught in the wind off the sea,

shipment of radioactive materials,
health implications,
Smear Meter, that sort of stuff
printed on pages ripped out,

radiological half life, atmos-
pheric dispersal,
Gamma-fields, Carbon-14,
blown through the dead silent Borough.

These who have never lived, blind lives so mean they
envy all others,
caitiffs whose deep-wailing plaints,
horrible outcries, hoarse sighs,
Even in duff weather I'd rather do a
skipper than stop there –
trouble of kiphouses is
vermin and no privacy.
piercing the starless air, dark-stained, dolent;
when I remember,
terror still bathes me in sweat –
their thunderous outbreathing of woe.
Hundreds of beds and the blankets is never
changed off the last one –
crabs, you can pick up like that.
No fucking plugs in the sinks.
From the tormented Sad, sigh-troubled breath a-
rises around them,
crowds that are many and great,
children and women and men.
Bloke in the next bed to me (I could see him)
pissed in his pillow
then he just slep on it wet.
Some on em masturbates, loud.
Let us not speak of them, merely observe and
silently pass by.

Isotope	
I-131	
Cs-137	
Sr-90	
Ru-106	910 rad lung dose to a 6 month old child

inversion ...

the present Lecture, the cloud-dosag
5 x 10^{-5} curie-sec/metre^3. Therefor
dosage of gamma activity would be

$$2{\cdot}011 \times 10^6 \times 5 \times 10^{-}$$

The dose from a semi-infinite cloud w
according to formula (2). From figur
size of the cloud is 0·38. Hence the
cloud would be

$$25 \times 0{\cdot}$$

Again, from Table II of Lecture No. 6
be 0·521 x 10^6 curie-MeV. Therefore
filters which retained all the iodine
gamma radiation dose would be reduced

EXTERNAL RADIATION FROM ACTIVITY DEPO

a radiological half life of 5700 years.
a long, long time. Carbon-14 emits a

After the meths she was honking and honking –
        front of the frayed mac
    stippled with vegetal bits,
    Surgical Spirit-beslimed.

In between honks she was screaming and screaming –
        someone has dragged her
    out of the derry back door,
    dumped her where we piss and shit.
    Now we can all get some kip.

or at least seems very likely, that he was given, we do not know by whom, a parcel of 'inside' papers relating to safety procedures during reactor damage and the 'black dust' scare. Since the authorities regarded all matters concerning environmental contamination as Official Secrets, the author's possession and publication (albeit in a form artistically metamorphosed) of certain of these documents was something of a risk. He steadfastly maintained to the police that he had found the material in a trash bucket on the Victoria Line station where he was busking.

That he was now physically and financially derelict ('No stranger to the unstemmable welter of shit') seems to have concentrated his notion of the 'slurry-wallowing degraded dispossessed' as a metaphor for all of *H. sapiens* involuntarily subjected to that other 'excreta' and thereby, irrespective of position in society, dispossessed of

Outside Victoria Station a quorum of
        no-hoper foetid
impromptu imbibers is causing a shindy:
        one of the number,
clutching a bottle of Thunderbird, half-full,
        rolls amongst litter
(chip-papers, Pepsi cans, Embassy packets –
        Indian take-out
   remnants adhere to her mac);
   under one arm is a crutch
   (the other is lopped at the elbow);
plaster encases her leg, which a colleague
        (sipping a Carlsberg)
kicks periodically, bellowing 'fugg-bag,
        fuggbagging fugg-bag'.

RADIATION PROTECTION TRAINING CO

1. Radiation Protection

7. Contamination Control

1. Personnel Movement Control

INTRODUCTION

Radioactive contamination may spread f
another in various ways. One of the princi
moving into a contaminated area and trackin
material on their clothing, shoes and perso
Various movement control techniques have ev

title **RADIATION EMERGENCY PROCEDURES**

Hazard Identification

radiation hazards present in the shutdow..
those normally present and those having p
ng retubing activities, are:

Ambient Gamma-fields

nt Gamma-fields are found within the reac
l shutdown conditions. These fields resu
ated components and fuel within the react
mination residing on the interior of pip

Radiation Beams Originating from the

gical shielding normally provides effec
iated with the activated in-core compo
as intense as 300 R/H, may emanate fr
al of a shield plug (S/P) from or of a

Radiation Fields Originating fror
Components and Fuel Removed from

Newspaper, wrapped round the torso between the
fourth and fifth jerseys
(night attire proper for doing a skipper in
icy December
under the Festival Hall),
carries a note to the Editor, from 'Ex-
Soldier' of Telford,
outlining plans to withdraw
DHSS cash from those
no-fixed-abode parasites.

Wound round a varicose indigo swollen
leg, between second
and third pair of trousers (which stink –
urine and faeces and sick),
Property Pages delineate *bijou*
River-View Flatlets
£600,000 each.

How much promethium remains?
Has there been tritium used?

Why did the PM deny there was any
contamination?
How do they mean to assure
home-owners no risk remains?

What was the level of contamination?
Where had it come from?
What is a 'Low Level' leak?
Why was the public not told?

Why has the PM consistently issued
flagrant denials
that any toxin remains
after these secret 'events'?

These are the questions which residents meant to
raise at the Meeting,
had it materialised.

113

of the Bottle-Bank cocktail. As we guzzled this mixture of stuff from the empties (shaken up in a wine bottle – a bit sour but OK, only it made us sick afterwards) he said he used to work at some atomic power station (quite posh, he was) but he got the sack for telling the newspapers about some radio-active leak, and he'd stolen all these papers – Top-Secret – from the Power Station, and he couldn't get work and then his wife died (cancer) so he came to this. I think he was fucking well crackers, but we all

Week of continuous Blue,
total amnesia, no recollection of
date or condition,
skipper or kiphouse or spike,
contusion and blood on the scalp,
spew, epilation, the squits,
sight as through flawed glass, misted, contorted,
nuns from St Mungo's
doling out dry bread and soup,
Mucky Preece skinning a cat
(bashed-in its head with a brick)
to add to the vegetal stew
bubbling up in the bucket,
swayingly unzips and waggles his penis,
smirched with the cat's gore,
urinates into the face of a Blessed
Sister of Mercy.

[And don't think it couldn't be *you*:
grievously wounded veteran of the
Battle of Bottle,
jobless, bereft of home, skint,
down in the cold uriniferous subway
spattered with drooled spawl,
lying in layers of newspaper ironies –
Property Prices,
smug To the Editor platitudes on The
Vagrancy Issue,
ads for Gonzalez Byass;
dosser with Top Man carrier-bag, en-
swathed in an *FT*
Gizzera quiddora fiftyfer fuggsay,
bankrupted, I been,
fugginwell bankrupted, me;
dolent, the wail from the Tube;
and don't think it couldn't be *you*.]

and 'morose old hypochondriac', as one reviewer dubbed his literary persona – which projected affectation was to become increasingly the reality.

During those last months of inebriate degeneracy (spent under the concrete span of a flyover, in an abandoned skip and in a defunct fibreglass storage bunker – sometime repository of the Borough's rock-salt for icy winter streets), the burden of his monody, rarely coherent, seems to have been Black Dust, 'Pancake' Contamination Meters, Smear Meters, Clean Zones and stochastic risk and *most startling penthouse £2,500,000*

RIVER
VIEWS
FROM
£123,500

VELVET CURTAINS

Sheds

KENNELS

MAINTENANCE FREE
STORAGE CONTAINERS

Back of the Maximart, Saturday evenings:
sometimes they chuck out
edibles (Sell By or Best Before dates of
which have expired –
Cheese 'n' Ham Tasties, Swiss Rolls,
Ready-to-Microwave-Burgers)
into a skip in the alley.
Tonight it is minty ice-cream.

Icy December: three rank expendables
squat on a split tomb
covered in carroty spew,
one has his cock loose and pisses all over him-
self and his colleagues –
steam from both this and their breaths.
Each grasps a 2-litre polythene tub from
which is extracted
scoopings of green ice by black half-mooned fingers.
Slurping and beard-smirch,
guzzle and emerald puke,
punctuate pulls from the communal Blue of
methyl amnesia.

Wind that disperses the Cloud is a blow for
Federalism,
fairly enfolding Muskovite, minaret,
Einkaufszentrum.

Scoffing our tea, bread-and-marge and secreted
surgical spirit
here in the crypt of St Botolph's it feels like a
fallout-shelter.

Inadequate Radiation Protection

Functional Disturbance of the Gut Fo

After irradiation of the gut in following disturbances of general fu: one to two hours:

(1) Nausea and vomiting

This might be thought of as a "r which stomach contents are dispo handled by the normal digestive bably originates in the brain.

(2) Diarrhoea

This is also a rejection phenome mechanisms.

it was discovered that some of the staff
oject had radioactive contamination on their
estigation it became evident that this form
tected by our "Pancake" contamination meters,
"smear" meters, but not by our older field
foot monitors, nor by the portal monitors.

Please find attached a status report
place
number of workers on the Large Scale
had contamination on their skin and c
the hand and foot monitors

Carbon-14 Contamination Problem

Melted-down boot polish, eau de Cologne, meths,
        surgical spirit,
    kerosine, car diesel, derv...

When the St Mungo lot roll up with hot soup,
        what you should do is
    keep back the slice of dry bread;

after they've fucked off, plaster the one side
        thick with the Brasso –
    goes down a regular treat.

    After a gobble of meths,
    crunch up a Trebor Mint fast –
    takes off the heat and the taste.

Piled in a ruck in the tundra a tump of
          Geigering reindeer...

Meanwhile the trains with their sinister finned flasks
          carrying spent rods
     hurtle perpetually on
through the benighted cities where trash a-
          masses and loonies,
alcos and other misfortunates make dole,
          one of whom ventures:
     I think this planet is fucked;
     not just me but the whole planet, fucked.

117

that she was into the lot – she
kept on about H and Coke and D.D.A.s
and skin-popping and main-lining
and then, when we started to have this
stew I'd made out of the rotten vegetables
they throw away off the stalls in the
market, she threw up straight in
the fire – we'd got a fire going in
the derry, made out of all the
banisters in the house. Then
someone shouted that the Bailiffs
were coming with the dozers,
and we got all the rats that we'd
killed, and got ready to chuck
them at those bastards with the

Legions of comatose owners of nothing
            under the concrete
      arches are juddered awake,
      impotent, dolent, bereft –

      radioactive spent rods,
bound for reprocessing from the reactors,
            carried in finned flasks,
rumble by railway by night through a city
            hugely unconscious.

      Nothing can ever be done;
      things are intractably thus;
knowing the bite of grief, all will be brought to
            destiny's issue;
those having precognition suffer
            sorrow beforehand.

Grief-bitten impotent owners of nothing,
            holding opinions
      gagged, disregarded, unsought.

Something is in the wind: terrible storms, an
absence of ozone,
huge decommission of plants,
delapse and delapse and delapse...

10,000 undesired drums
(3,800 tonnes)
abandoned four-high in a rickety stack that
pops with expansion,
sizzles and bubbles and fumes
fizzing from leaks in the rust
in the full glare of the sun
200 yards from a shanty camp's tetrous ex-
pendable tosspots,
scumbags and alcos and bums.

how the author was last encountered in the concourse of Euston, pediculous, intoxicated beyond capability, plunging and bucking like a demented warhorse – the side of the head oftentimes cracking against the tiled floor, blood and contusion already in evidence, a (profoundly embarrassed and irritated) companion struggling to hold

Council blokes pulled down the derry and then set
        fire to the floorboards,
rafters and anything else that would burn (the
        squatters of course had
    already burnt all the doors,
    banisters, skirtingboards, stairs).

Those who had formerly dossed there returned that
        night to the bonfire,
Mucky Preece found an old bucket and stewed up
        veg which the market
stallholders chuck in the gutters because it's
        rotten or damaged –
    onions, a turnip, some sprouts.
    The embers were glowing for days.

That's where they found it, singed to the waist, its
        charcoaly leg-sticks
(one of which must have been smashed and remained en-
        cased in cast plaster)
    stuck in still-fulminant ash,
    bits of veg puked on the mac,
    blue meths clutched tight in one claw,
    other limb lopped at the elbow.

Wind that disperses the Cloud (a blow for De-
        mocracy) favours
Palace twerp, propertied yuppie and news-wrapped
        dosser with doses
equal in Geiger croaks. Shreds of (marked **Secret**)
        papers are scuttering
    over the wrecked party-lawn's
    panic-vacated marquee
    and under the Festival Hall,
    drift against cheap sleeping-bags,
    cardboard, plonk bottles and stiffs:

rads,

stront,

risk,

leak,

contam

Health Implications

Based on the risk estimates
can be concluded that the ri
cancer after irradiation to
from negative to an upper bc
year per rem (Section 2.1).
mulation of extremity dose t
lifetime, it can be shown th
skin cancer is 2.4 x 10^{-5} pe
risk, based on the 5% case-f
1.2 x 10^{-6} per rem which is
of the total stochastic risk
Therefore, our calculation i
ICRP's skin weighting factor

function

OPERATING MANUAL

...ned, int... ...t. Some deaths in ... weeks, possible eventual death of 50% of individuals for about 450 rads.

Nausea, vomiting, diarrhea in first hours. Short latent period followed by diarrhea, hemorrhage, purpura, inflammation of throat, fever by end of first week. Rapid emaciation, and death as early as 2nd week with possible eventual death of 100% of exposed individuals.

approved by

Carrying on as though nothing is wrong is
what we are good at:
incontrovertible end;
shrieks, lamentations and dole;
lost livers, roof-trees and hearths;
on the waste ground at the back of the factory
there's a crone scumbag
that kips in a big cardboard box,
etiolated and crushed;
those having precognition suffer
madness beforehand
**(Efforts are now being made to encase in
concrete the...)**; meanwhile,
here is a factory daily producing
thousands of badges
emblazoned with **Have a Nice Day**.

Dusty, crepuscular, vast;
ranks of unfortunate supines fading
into infinity;
chamber or bunker or vault
seemingly lacking extremities; coughing,
puking, diarrhoea;
drone of the crazy invisible exe-
getist intoning
Woe vnto woe vnto woe
vnto woe vnto woe vnto woe

squit
rads

honk
stront

piss
risk

moths
leak

dis tress
con tam

SHITHEADS

(1989)

[Squirrelprick Press is producing his latest (a light intermezzo),
Shitheads, a thing of great charm; hand-deckled, Limited, limp.]

Designatory

Ours is that thriving company noted for
caps (worn by prankster drolls) on the peaks of which,
gleaming, repose the simulacra,
sculpted in plastic, of great big dog turds.
Thus are we designated: **Shitheads.**

Holidaywise

Aspirant big-time publican (nagged by
termagant tart spouse)
flies for the golf to Costa del Parvenu
where are encountered:
Chicken 'n' Turkey Chunks chief
(puffing Habanas like mad);
name-dropping, aitch-dropping rep
('Sundries and Fancy Goods, me');
Nearly New Motor Cars baron whose slattern
wife is a quondam
Tiller Girl tap-dancer trull;
yuppie computer exec...

Translationese

Junior Executive Computer Manager [*sic*], it isn't that I am coy about using your real name (Kydd), my dear, damp-eared callow fellow, but that I suspect my readers, ignorant unsophisticates!, of never having even heard of you! Can you imagine that?! No, of course you can't. How I respect your grey suit's delicate stripe; how I admire your *savoir vivre* when you light up another of those slim panatellas; how impressed I am by your shinily-polished slipper-like shoes (tasteful, with their little gold tassels!); how I wish that I had a slimline leatherette brief-case, like yours, with *my* initials on it. I assure you that I was *not* alluding to *you* when I wrote: 'opinionated whippersnappers tinker with Hi-Tech'; 'ill-read mediocrities are catapulted to positions of grandeur for which they are grotesquely inadequate'. Poor young chap, whom I so much esteem, you have dashed yourself slap-bang into this slab of hard-edged prose.

Managerial

Smith (a sobriquet much in vogue with con-men)
and your Board of Directors, bumpkin straw-heads,
and your quorum of exec greysuit shysters
[whose sub-literacy ensures my safety],
you have earned our esteem in these blunt hendecs;
for your management of us (six years, thank you)
systematically has reduced our travail
and secured us a future wholly workless.

Englished

XXXIII

O Vibennius *pater*, best of bath-house
petty-larcenists, and your pervert offspring
(for the father's the one whose right hand's fouler,
while the son's got a more voracious arsehole),
why not go into exile, some vile region? –
since you may as well, now that father's thefts are
universally known of, nor can you, son,
not at any price, tout those bristly buttocks.

XL

Little Ravidus, what sad brain disturbance
makes you fling yourself into my sharp spiked verse?
What misguidedly-invoked god, raised rashly,
is preparing to rouse a crazy dispute?
Or you'd maybe just like your name made public?
What's the matter, eh? You want fame at all costs?
You shall have it then, since you've shown a fancy
to love *my* love – and you'll pay yearly for it.

XLIII

Good day, lady with not the least of noses,
with no elegant ankle, nor dark sloe-eyes,
nor un-slobbering lips, nor long fine fingers,
nor, quite clearly, an *over*-urbane diction,
friend of swindling bankrupt Formianus.
Does your pitiful province laud your beauty?
Do they dare to compare you with our Lesbia?!
O this era of tasteless, witless folly!

LXXIX

Lesbius is good-looking – what of it? Lesbia chooses
him in preference to you, Catullus, and all of your tribe.

Yet, if this dandy can muster three { blessings / kisses } from genuine worthies,
Catullus, and all of his tribe, will own themselves utterly sold.

LXXXIX

Gellius is slender – and why not? – he's got such a marvellous mother,
such a fine, healthy, robust, sister of such comely charm,

such a good uncle [in charge of them], everywhere bulging with maiden
relatives – so from what cause could he be other than gaunt?

Since he'll not handle anything other than that which is outlawed,
you'll learn, as much as you wish, the reason why he is lean.

XCIII

I'm not over-sedulous, Caesar, in trying to win your approval,
nor do I seek to enquire if you're a white man or black.

CIII

Please be so kind as to let me have back my ten sesterces, Silo,
thereafter, as much as you like, be un-housetrained, un-broken-in;

or, if the lucre so pleases you, keep it, but then be so kind as
to refrain from being a boor, untamed barbarian, pimp.

Managerial

Thanks, Mr Smith, for deciding *Execly*, when you abandoned
people and purchased a car – just over 13 grand
(humans depreciate more).

Company limos, especially this one (a silver *Montego*),
ego-boost Reps and Execs, heighten the tone of the place.

That day you also saw fit to lay-off three hapless employees:
millworker, driver, a clerk – also-rans not worth three fucks.

Vagrants

Twenty-three Black Country ramblers, thank you
(plenty of decibels, Brummagem blah-blah,
Army Stores walking-boots, anoraks, knapsacks,
one of you wearing a **Have a nice day** badge,
one of you wearing a cap blazoned **Shithead**,
one of you chucking a drained 7-Up can into the heather)

for cheering this lonely Shropshire upland
with orange and crimson fluorescent clobber,
shrieks, squeals, ululations and feculent litter
(tampons and turds smirch bracken and whins), and for
driving away the only Hen Harrier seen in ten years here.

EVAGATORY

(1992)

Doyle's on the harbour, dusk, pulse of warning light,
octopus, crayfish, chill gold dry semillon's
bouquet of ripe grapes/pollen; plum-mauve
Rothko of afterglow on which silent
slow-flapping fruit-bats' transient silhouettes...

a.m., a carcinogenic sunrise
(15% of population...),
shrieking, an iridescence of lorikeets
raucous from palms and blossoming eucalypts;
Sydney, *The Age* screwed up in a trash-bucket.

8 a.m., Hobart, bar of the Ship Hotel.
Over their ice-cold Cascades a couple of
shicks are discussing Nubeena, Wedge Bay,
Oakwood, Port Arthur, Highcroft, Stormlea,
how, in the Convict Ruins, wylahs
(yellow-tailed black, funereal cockatoos,
Calyptorhynchus funereus),
wailing their weird *wee-yu wy-la*, are
really the ghosts of sun-charred hanged cons.

Tew that kindley Chaplaing
whot preechis in Port After:
Sir, I gets hangd this day,
me as wus transportud
back in '37
(then ajed onley 16)
tew New Serf Wails, escaped,
become bushranjer, catched,
sent Port After, neerly
scaped agin – this time
sent Nofuck Isle, rebelld,
sentenst tew be hangd.
But I was wonce humayne,
drove tew desparayshun
by crewelty of prizzin.
Strong ties of erth wil soon
be renched, this burnin fever
of life wil soon be kwenched,
mi grayve wil be a haven,
a restern plays fer me,
Wil Westwood, sir, from cup
of mizry hav I drank
from 16th yeer, ten long
yeeers, the sweetest drarft
is that as takes away
mizry of livin deth.
I welcum deth – a frend
as do deceyve no man –
and all shall then be qiyet,
no tyrant wil disturb
repoze, I hope. I now
do bid the world A Due
and all as it contaynes!

Pipe Clay Lagoon, wet silver ellipse of sand
pulsing in lightwaves, pure cerulean dome,
    indigo-bruised smooth straits of turquoise,
bloodshot-eyed *Larus novaehollandiae*,

delicacies laid out on a linen cloth,
    crusty bread, avocados, smoked quails,
        crisp knots of lettuce, terrine of salmon,
    raspberries, pinot noir Moorilla,

resinous pine shade under an ozone hole
    (one of those routine periodic
faunal extinctions [cf. the Cambrian]),
    eucalypts shred-barked, parched buff hectares.

26 hours of 747-lag,
touchdown to Greenhouse meteorology,
        wind preternatural, pissing acid.

    Down from the sleet-clad mountains into
        Mostar, fecundity (pulsing UV
    irradiating vines, figs, peaches).

    Carp baked in herbs and bijelo vino,
carcass of whole lamb spiked on a slow-turned spit
over sweet pine-smoke outside a crumbling bar.

    Long after midnight, crno vino,
    visokokvalitetno vino,
        vinjak, strings strummed by a frost-haired elder,
Jasmina mouthing soft-breathed translationese:

This is his song's weight, Time's malice castigates
    not only me (whose beard grows snow-hued,
    bones become joint-sore, dulled eyes gum-filled),
        also fair governments, concepts, zeniths,
    all which we valued nears expiry.

Midnight, an open window in Trebinje,
  thrashing of warm May rain on fig leaves,
nightingale, one hour richly mellifluous
    under this vitriolated downpour.

      Café Dalmacija, Adriatic
  violet (dark as crno vino),
  liquorice-bitter gritty coffee,
vinjac, Jasmina's whispered translation of
      lyrical twang from a grizzled oldie:

  Surely Odysseus roamed these blithe isles,
parsley and iris cushioning meadowlands,
fumous the scents of split cypress, juniper,
vine-stems rich-clustered, temptress voluptuous,
      touched by salacious caresses [silence,
scanning with tears a barren expanse of sea],
knowing delights venereal, lachrymose.

ye haue heard this yarn afore
(but I'm minded on it againe
thefe daies of fqualls and rank clouds
and raines as is vitriolic –
pines fhorn ftark as mizzen-mafts
wi neuer a frolicfome fowl –
and ye top-gallant air all rent):

how we was one Monday anchored
off Mafcarenhas Iflande
in fourteen fathom o water;
how, feeking diuerfion, we landed;
how, on ye trees, there was pigeons
as blue as polifhed flate

which fuffered vs, being fo tame,
for to pluck em iuft like fruits
from ye branches and pull their necks;
how we killed two hundred firft day;
how we alfo killed grey paraquets
(moft entertayninge to cetch
a grey paraquet and *twift* it
fo as it fqueals aloud
till ye reft of its kind flock round,
therevpon themfelues being cetched);
how there was alfo penguins
(which laft hath but ftumps for wings,
fo being ye eafier to kill)
which we killed above four hundred;
how there was alfo wild geefe
and turtles above an hundred;
how we killed all thefe and more;
and ye Tuefday more and more;
and ye Wednefday more and more;
and ye Thurfday more and more;
ye haue heard this yarn afore

Came to an island farctate with feculence:
chip-papers, Diet-Pepsi cans clattering,
prams, supermarket trolleys, spent mattresses,

bus-rank of steel and rank uriniferous
concrete, a footbridge richly enlivened with
   aerosol squirtings, daubed graffiti,

        pustular simian sub-teenagers
   hurling abuse and empty bottles
        over the parapet into crowds of
        pensioners waiting for **X-PRESS SERVISS**,

        xylophone tinkle of smashed glass, crackle
   under a tyre, a hapless old fart
   stanching the flow from freshly sliced flesh.

Avian botulism thriving
(black plastic bin-bags/scavenging *Laridae*);
sand-eels depleted (over-fishing):

sanitised quondam herring gull colony,
sanitised quondam kittiwake colony –
all that remains, their last year's shit's stink.

53 bus approaching the terminus;
dapper sartorial English elder
suited in Manx tweed, close-clipped grey tash:

Too much is wrong, Gibbonian undertones,
schooling and bread and dress and manners,
era's decline, Elgarian sadnesses;

too much is wrong, duff ticker, insomnia,
ulcer and thyrotoxicosis,
end of the world in one's lifetime likely,
flight of a sparrow brief through the feasting hall.

Perilous trek, unarmed, unaccompanied:
set out from Cranium, through uncharted
swamp, to arrive at Lingua Franca,
thence to this Logaoedic Dependency.

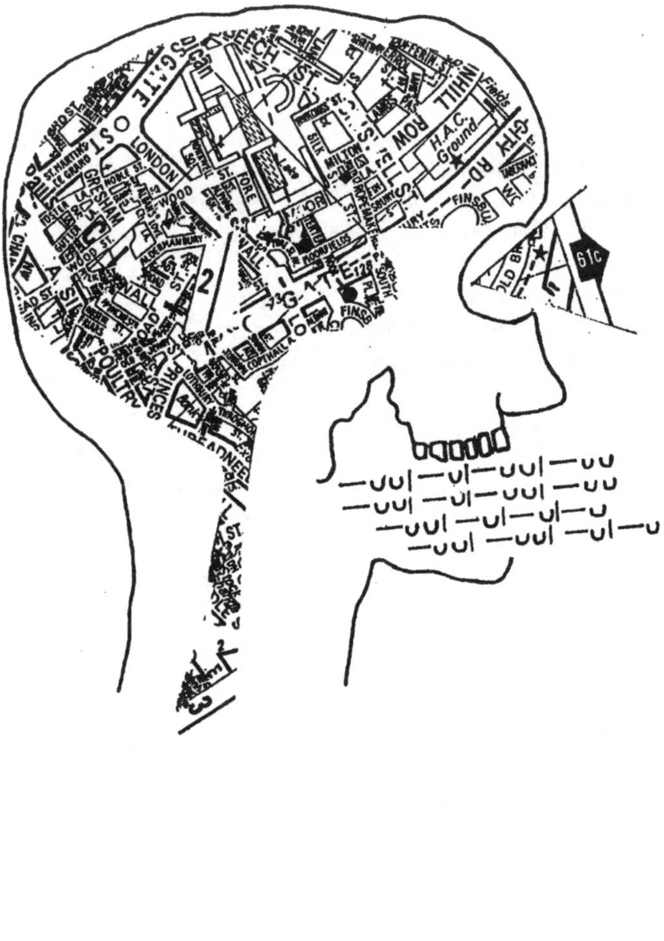

Cranial voice loquacious/inadequate
   (translationese from life to lingo):

Only a troubled idyll now possible,
pastoral picnic under an ozone hole,
England, *The Times* screwed up in a trash-bucket,
   gliding astern, the Thames, the old prides,
   end of an era, nation, notion,
      Albion urban, devenustated
   (one of those routine periodic
faunal extinctions [cf. the Permian]),
arthropod aberration (posterity).

a dreadful, bloody, civil insurrection among the poor mad islanders brought about because their automobiles, which they had revered above all else, and which had helped boost their weak, inferior egos, had been confiscated by their (suddenly aware and panic-stricken) government. For it seems that, whereas the manifest absurdity of mayhem on congested tarmac and the lowering mantle of ferruginous fog had somehow failed to awaken authoritarian sensibility, this abrupt (albeit long-prognosticated) termination of a fundamental, unrenewable

Newspapers there (the sumps of society,
draining off, holding up for inspection a
   corporate concentrated slurry)
retail, with relish, mayhem and muck of a
      clapped-out, subliterate, scrap-stuffed fake state:
   23.3 million vehicles,
   29.8 million drivers,
300 000 maimed on their ludicrous
   tarmac p.a., 5000 flenched dead –
      fortunate, then, that it doesn't matter
(for they are far too philoprogenitive).

Snow-haired, an elder, dulled eyes gum-filled,
tuning a sweet-toned curious instrument,
gulps from a goblet of local merlot,
sings on a theme whose fame was fabled,
that of a sad realm farctate with feculence
(patois and translationese alternately):

Gobschighte damapetty,
gobby Fer-dama,
getspeeke baggsy,
getspeeke parly
comma cul, comma
malbicker-bicker,
porky getspeeke?, porky?

Wonderful little Madam,
self-mocking Iron Lady,
who some said was a windbag,
some said talked
like an arsehole, like
a termagant – why,
why did some say that?

Pascoz vots clobberjoli,
vots chevvy-dur dur,
vots baggsymain chic,
vots collier-prick,
cuntyvach twitnit,
iscst pukkerjoli –
illos jalouz dats porky!

Because your pretty frocks,
your permed-stiff hair,
your smart handbag, your
tight-sharp necklace,
satrapess so marvellous,
were so beautiful –
they were envious, that's it!

Ni iscst vots marrypappa
grignaleto, ne.
Mas vots pollytiq
saggio sauvay
vots salinsula,
insulapetty,
et fair tutts egal mit-nochts.

Nor was your spouse
a pipsqueak – far from it!
But your many wise policies
were saving your islet,
your filthy isle, and
made all equal with nil.

East End of London, where the indigenous
practise a noteworthy brand of homicide –
fruit and veg hurled from speeding limos.
Melons, potatoes, cauliflowers, aubergines,
clutter the vegetarian headlines here:
Turnip tops septuagenarian shopper,
Juvenile jogger culled by cabbage.

Forest, Sarawak, limestone outcrop,
caverns of roosting Bornean horseshoe bats
(faeces of which are sifted by cockroaches);

one-and-a-half miles into the labyrinth,
reservoir, stalactitic vaulting,
etiolated, eyeless crustacean,
wheeze of a Tilley lamp near expiry.

Guideless, directionless, lightless, silence.

Edge of black Baltic, night, north-easter,
low-ceilinged candle-lit gloomy *keller*,
flocculent-headed yeast-fragrant beer, a bench,
basins of pork-dripping, course sour rye-bread,
Germanic drone of a drunk salt's slurred dirge,
whisper of scented soft-breathed translationese:

Mine is a sea-borne sorrowful history,
winters of toil through tempests, foam frosts,
fearing the future's vicious voyage,
lashing of iced brine, hurled hail, waves' thrash,
longing for land and cuckoo's sad call of spring...

nothing on earth can abide forever,
illness or age or aggression takes us,
striving for fame beyond death is futile
(none will be left to celebrate heroes' *lof*),

days and delights depart, and inferior
beings infest and despoil earth, each one
greys and grows grave and, pallid, passes.

...dawn of each day I bewail my sorrows,
how I was sundered in youth from homelands

[fuelled by a yeast-frothed litre, a wandering
dosser drones on in the local lingo],

no man grows wise without many winters spent
pondering folly of worthless world's-gear,

awful the apprehension of earth-ending,
crumbled the mead-hall, no laugh lasting,

where are the heroes, word-hoarders, feasting-feats? –
gone back to dark as though they had never been,

life is a loan and bank accounts transient,
kindred are skewered on sharp-spiked ash-spears,

all of this world will be Weird-wreaked,
emptied...

Province of hyperborean bleakness,
Cranium. Roused by nightmare (in which
I am a butcher, cleaver repeatedly
hacking your carcass, five-years-dead friend),
grief gushes raw again from an old lesion.

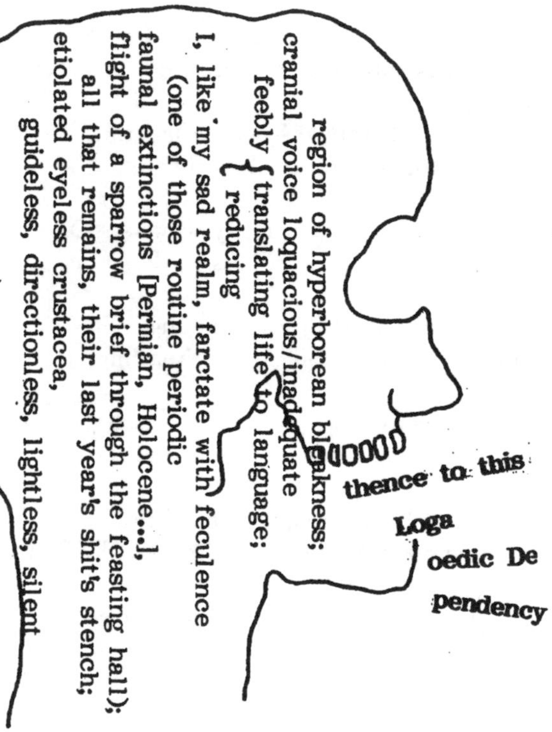

upon an island where the natives venerated a deity. It was soon apprehended that the object of their adoration was a species of duck, *Anas platyrhynchos* (the mallard). Anyone unenlightened enough to revere, say, the pochard (*Aythya ferina*), the wigeon (*Anas penelope*) or the smew (*Mergus albellus*) was subjected to corrective interrogation by a most venerable committee and, invariably, sentenced to suffer personal destruction.

There was one in that place, cowering in the police-protected exile of a concrete bunker, who had advocated, ill-advisedly, the omniscient immutability of the velvet scoter (*Melanitta fusca*), and

Prouerbes xiij. iij

He that infults Our Mallard muft pay for it;
hee that reueres falfe pochard and blafphemous
wigeon and fmew knows not Y^e^ True Quack
which was reuealed to vs by Our Drake's beak.

Therefore a Iiffy bag plump with correctiue plaftic explofiue
plops on ye mat with ye mail, blafts his child's face into pulp.

[Hee who keeps fhtum ftays aliue.]

Waded ashore, St Pancras Isle, 2 a.m.,
knee-deep in poly burger-boxes,
black plastic bin-bags, spat snot, spilt pils.

Cushioned in mulch from trash-skips' spillage
(cabbage fronds, glass shards, date-expired cakes),
calmly a couple coited, stirred by
conviviality [or copecks].

Came to an island whereon the natives make
caps (worn by prankster drolls) on the peaks of which,
gleaming, repose the simulacra,
sculpted in plastic, of great big dog turds.
Thus are they designated: **Shitheads**.

Sham-rustic lair of quondam Parnassian
(lapsed into silence – like great Sibelius,
mute till the end – reflective of wordlessness);

vinous-rich wallflowers, arbour, a wicker chair
in the last corner receiving sunlight;
evening, a violet-shadowed sad shire
running to exponential ruin
(not enough condoms, too many mountain bikes);

voice in the head loquacious/inadequate
glibly enumerating mayhem
(prettily pyrotechnic oilfields,
Cape Grim recording ozone-depleting air,
progeny guaranteed a climacteric);

only a troubled idyll now possible,
few of the better years remaining...
'55 Margaux, '61 Léoville.

Blizzard, Niagara, roaring white-out,
cast iron scrolls of parapet frozen like
ammonite whorls in waxed ice matrix.

Mountainous Franco-ltalian border,
Tende, medieval, steep labyrinthine wynds,
bell-tower surmounting rough terracotta-roofed
hovels, a terraced graveyard, tombs like
hundreds of matrices pierced with snap-shots.

Our craft approaching ye fhore,
many fcores of diuers fowls,
all clagged in fome fticky tar,
did flacker away from ye land;
foon we was able to fee
ye aquatic graffes all fered,
likewife all nature of flora;
fifhes vp-bellied and white
in a noifome vifcous fwell,
for, in truth, ye waues was black,
ye furface a floating fcum;
on running athwart a ridge
of rock, when we feared our fkiff
muft fpring a breach in her caulk,
rather, ye fable stone
did crumble like iet meringue;
now preternatural fqualls
did moderate, and ftrange vapours
defcend in ferruginous fog,
an oppreffiue heat, withal;
then did we verily know
we had entered vnto Y^e Gulph.

region of hyperborean bleakness;
cranial voice loquacious/inadequate
feebly { translating life to language;
reducing
I, like my sad realm, farctate with feculence
(one of those routine periodic
faunal extinctions [Permian, Holocene…],
flight of a sparrow brief through the feasting hall,
all that remains, their last year's shit's stench),
etiolated eyeless crustacean,
etiolated aberration,
guideless, directionless, lightless, silent

[cranial voice gratuitous/garrulous:]

region of hyperborean bleakness;
region of hyperborean bleakness;
region of hyperborean bleakness;
cranial voice loquacious/inadequate
cranial voice loquacious/inadequate
cranial voice loquacious/inadequate
feebly { translating life to language;
feebly { translating life to language;
feebly { translating life to language;
reducing
reducing
reducing
I, like my sad realm, farctate with feculence
I, like my sad realm, farctate with feculence
I, like my sad realm, farctate with feculence
(one of those routine periodic
(one of those routine periodic
(one of those routine periodic
faunal extinctions [Permian, Holocene...],
faunal extinctions [Permian, Holocene...],
faunal extinctions [Permian, Holocene...],
flight of a sparrow brief through the feasting hall);
flight of a sparrow brief through the feasting hall);
flight of a sparrow brief through the feasting hall);
all that remains, their last year's shit's stench;
all that remains, their last year's shit's stench;
all that remains, their last year's shit's stench;
etiolated eyeless crustacea,
etiolated eyeless crustacea,
etiolated eyeless crustacea,
guideless, directionless, lightless, silent
guideless, directionless, lightless, silent
guideless, directionless, lightless, silent

[thence to this silence, total, Sibelian]
[thence to this silence, total, Sibelian]
[thence to this silence, total, Sibelian]

Midwinter feast, crammed stalls in a market-place;
        vendors of steaming gewürzy glühwein;
over a pine blaze, sputtering griddled wursts;
easterly sleet blast lashing the flanks of freak
beasts in a side-show – muzzled, incongruous
        Indian elephant, dromedary;

ratskeller clamour, warm odoriferous
    waftings from baked eel, roast goose, wildschwein
    basted with pears in portugieser;

babel of strange-tongued wanderers; slumping in
    schweinschmalz, a Northman, soused in weisswein,
        incomprehensibly stutters slurred dirge:

        Quondam Parnassian, muse prolific,
    Master of Troubled Idyll, charted
        province of hyperborean bleakness...
fell into silence, like great Sibelius
mute till the end, reflective of soundlessness.

All that remains, the stench of their excrement.

    sea-level newly pole-augmented,
        mutated arthropods, algae, UV,
force 12s dispersing disbound Collected Works

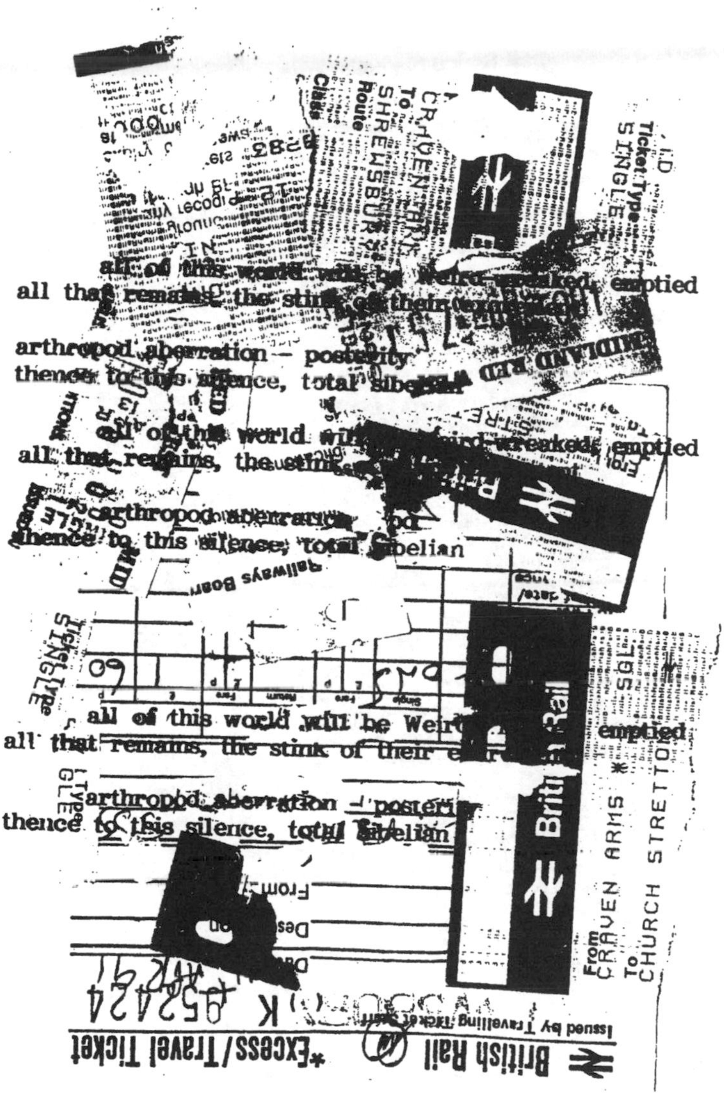
all of this world will be Weird wreaked, emptied
all that remains, the stink of their
arthropod aberration – posterity
thence to this silence, total
all of this world will be Weird wreaked, emptied
all that remains, the stink of their
arthropod aberration – posterity
thence to this silence, total
Ticket Type SINGLE
CRAVEN ARMS
To SHREWSBURY
Route
Class
MIDLAND RED
Railways Board
British Rail
From CRAVEN ARMS
To CHURCH STRETTON
SGL
British Rail
Issued by Travelling Ticket Staff
*Excess/Travel Ticket

... and is likely ...
craft to find the heliopause.

Voyager will be hurtling through space searching for the heliopause — the interface where the Sun's influence ends and interstellar space begins.

... explorers to cross this fence — by the year 2010 or 2020, when they may still have almost 10 years of contact with the Earth before they run out of power.

Voyager 1 after ...

This boundary marks the edge of the solar winds, where the energy and atomic particles streaming out from the Sun cease, and has never been ... Earth ...

Beyond the year 2020, the plutonium-based generators on board the spacecraft will give too little power to keep the Voyagers operating as explorers, but they will continue to hurtle through the Milky Way. In 40,000 years time, Voyager 1 will meet the star AC+79 3888, in the northern constellation of Camelopardalis.

... same time, Voyager ... will encounter Ross 248, and some 250,000 years later the star Sirius. But these "encounters" will be at distances of trillions of miles from the stars, rather than ... Voyager ...

... terms of science — particles we have never dreamed of. There ...

Sirius about twice as far away as Proxima Centauri — i.e. 8.6 light years — very nearby in cosmic terms only

1 LIGHT YEAR ≈ TEN MILLION MILLION KM.

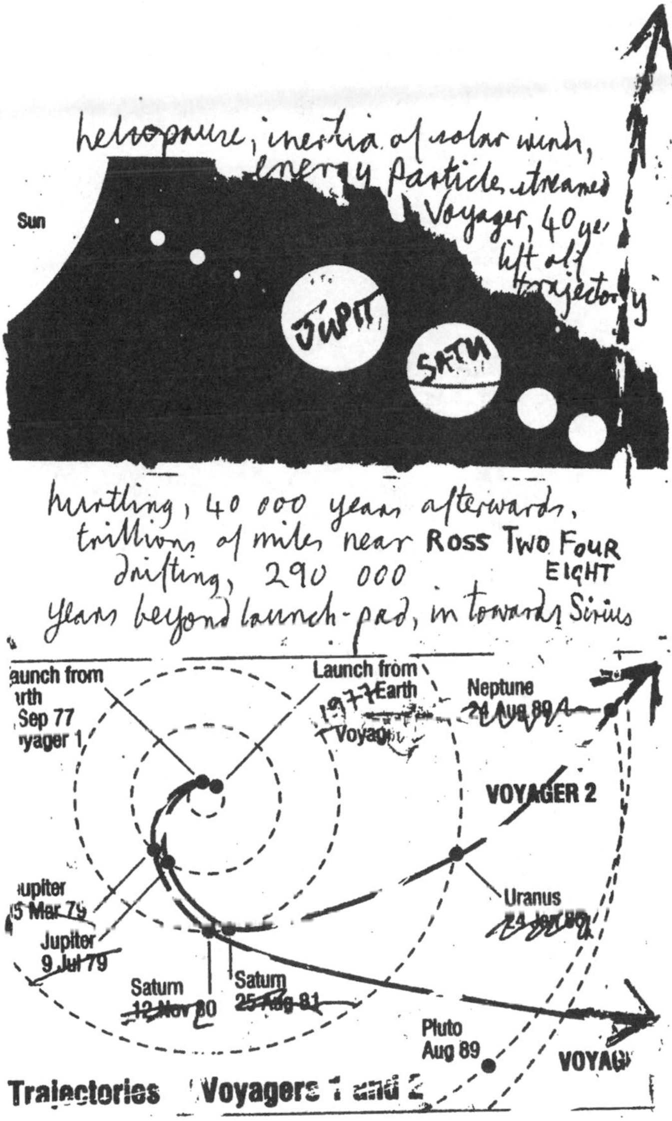
heliopause, inertia of solar winds,
energy particle streamed
Voyager, 40 ye
lift off
trajectory
Sun
JUPIT
hurtling, 40 000 years afterwards,
trillions of miles near ROSS TWO FOUR
EIGHT
drifting, 290 000
years beyond launch-pad, in towards Sirius
Launch from
Earth
Voyager 1
Launch from
1977 Earth
Neptune
VOYAGER 2
Uranus
Jupiter
Jupiter
9 Jul 79
Saturn
Saturn
Pluto
Aug 89
Trajectories Voyagers 1 and 2

heliopause, inertia of solar winds,
        energy particles streamed from Sun cease,
    Voyager, 40 years since lift-off,
        power from plutonium generator
greatly reduced, continues trajectory,

hurtling, 40 000 years afterwards,
    trillions of miles near Ross 248,

drifting, 290 000
years beyond launch-pad, in towards Sirius

LAST POEMS

(1994)

Foreword

These poems are printed in the order in which they were found (contained in an envelope bearing a superscription, in the author's hand, 'Last Poems', together with a holograph note indicating that the pieces 'Euripidean' and 'Thucydidean' should be ascribed to 'an anonymous cleric of the nineteenth century').

The sanguinary 'Ovidian' is a treatment, in two parts, of Ovid's *Metamorphoses* (IV. 663-803 and V. 1-235) done into Reading's characteristic quasi-classical hexameters. 'Homeric' is an adaptation, similarly rendered, of XXII. 381-477 from the *Odyssey*.

The poems entitled 'Funerary', 'Fragmentary' and 'Exilic' are evidently 'versions' of Anglo-Saxon pieces (respectively, the end of *Beowulf*, 'The Ruin' and 'The Wife's Lament'). 'Fates of Men' derives from a poem of that title in the *Exeter Book*.

'Erosive' and the untitled final two pages are reproduced as found. It is unclear whether the author intended them to appear in their present form, or whether they represent drafts towards an unrealised work in progress.

JOHN BILSTON,
Melaleuca, 1994.

[Untitled]

[wizened anhydrous frail wisps of laurel leaves,
rustle of old gratuitous scrivening,
pages of faded palimpsest hieroglyphs,
half-hidden/half-glimpsed sorrowful utterance,
sepia faded tremulous holograph,
crackle of brittle anhydrous laurel leaves,
sepia-scrivened crumbled eroded leaves,
parchment eroded round the sad utterance,
rotted the frail bond, with it the utterance,]

Funerary

Preparing a pyre,   the people of the Geats
hung round it helmets,   halberds and battle-dress;
lamenting, they laid   their lord in the midst of it.
High on the wold   his warriors kindled it,
wood-smoke whirled,   there was weeping, flames leapt.
After the wind's-rush,   the white-hot cadaver
fell into fragments.   Fear was expressed
by a Geatish woman   who wailed a keen
over the body,   bad times were forecast –
terror, killing,   captivity, shame.
The smoke was swallowed   by sky. On the headland
a barrow was built,   both broad and lofty,
a landmark for miles   to mariners. Ten days
later they finished it,   a fine memorial
for a man so mighty in martial conflict.
A vault was wrought   around his ashes.
Trappings, taken   from the treasure-hoard, next were
buried in the barrow –   bright gold entrusted
to earth, where it rests,   rusted, useless
as all world's-gear is.   Geatish princes
rode round the mound,   making great grief.

And this is fitting: for fair men to value
with powerful words their worthy lord
when his life, as all men's must, departs him.
So the men of the Geats, Great-Hall-dwellers,
who'd shared the hearth with the hero, bewailed,
claiming their king was the kindest of leaders,
the mildest of men, most meriting renown.

Regal

Mother was holding up a Pyrex pie-dish
(lined with plump apple lumps) in her left hand,
flopping the pastry lid on with her right,
trimming the droopy overlaps and jabbing
steam-vents. She wiped a floured hand on her apron
and tuned the wireless – what Roy Fuller calls
'Some inexplicable, imperial,
Elgarian sadness' filled the scullery:
His Majesty, King George VI, is dead.

The following year we single-filed from school
down to the flicks to see a double feature
(stark Everest surmounted by Tenzing,
and the Queen crowned). The Regal, I recall,
was gaudy, faded, had seen better days.

Euripidean

What we have long foretold will before long be
    fully accomplished, the theme of dirges.

Low, low it lies, imperial majesty,
vanished the pomp, the high-vaunted vanities,
  nothing remains, no name, no issue.

Mothers, expire with grief on beholding your
progeny thus deformed and your lovely ones
  now become loathsome, pallid, death-waxed.

  Hostile manipulator, Cronus,
  what need had I of sons or daughters?
This grievous fate should not have befallen me:
  children from these arms wrenched for ever.

  Not to be borne, such weight of anguish.

See, the audacious miscreants suffering.

'Wretch that I am! What cause is assignable
for such a chain of diresome calamities?'
Folly, towards which untutored man inclines;
  Sunk City's scum and pestilential
terrors, ascribe to gods unassuageable.

Nor may we now reach forth with our impotent
  hands to forestall our headlong downrush,
  having irrevocably acted.

    Some, there are, hold that the ills attending
  mankind exceed his joys; per contra,
others opine that his frail life encompasses
more bliss than woe – for how could he, otherwise,
  bear to endure each grief-racked orbit?

Bosnian

Sipping grit-coffee and vinjak outside a
bar in the Turkish
Quarter, observe how Hooded Crows crowd and
bicker for carrion
in the fast-darkening air grown rank with
barbecued lambs' smoke.

[Sarajevo, 1992]

Homeric

After Odysseus had slaughtered the Suitors he
grimly surveyed them –
sprawling in crans in a welter of blood and
muck, like the beached fish
dragged up by driftnetters onto the sand to
gulp for the grey brine
till in the heat of the sun they expire, so
lay the slain Suitors.

Calling Telemachus, devious-thinking
wily Odysseus
asked for the nurse Eurycleia to be brought
into his presence.

Rattling her door, Telemachus shouted
old Eurycleia,
matron in charge of the servant women, to
go to his father.

When she arrived, she discovered Odysseus
striding through corpses,
spattered with offal and gore, like a lion
leaving a farmstead
where he has feasted on cattle, the blood-gouts
staining his body.

When she set eyes on the dead and the blood-bath,
old Eurycleia
let out a triumphal yell but Odysseus
stopped her with these words:
'Silence, old woman, for it is immoral to
gloat over slain men;
justice was meted out to them by the
gods for their evil,
they have been slain for their want of respect, their
doom has been dreadful.

Now, let us talk of the women attendants –
who has betrayed me?'
'Sir, of the fifty who serve in your household
twelve should be punished
for their recalcitrance – even Penelope
couldn't control them.'
'Go to those women who flouted decorum;
summon them to me.'
These were his words, and the nurse was quick to
muster the culprits.

Meanwhile Odysseus briefed his son and his
two faithful herdsmen:
'Carry the carcasses out of here – order the
women to help you.
Then swab the elegant chairs and tables with
sponges and water.
Then, when the palace is cleansed and in order,
take out the women,
lead them between the domed outhouse and the
wall of the courtyard,
then with your long-bladed swords make sure you
hack them to pieces –
end their lascivious memories of lewd
nights with the Suitors.'

Howling, convulsively sobbing, the women were
  herded together.
Firstly they dragged out the carcasses, dumped them
  under the portal
(superintending, Odysseus forced their
  unwilling labour);
next, they attended to swabbing the elegant
  chairs and the tables;
meanwhile Telemachus worked with the pair of
  trustworthy herdsmen
scraping with shovels the crusted blood-clots
  out of the flooring,
ordered the women to carry away the
  loathsome detritus.

Now that the palace was cleansed and in order, the
  women were taken,
herded between the domed outhouse and the
  wall of the courtyard,
into a corner from which there could be no
  hope of escaping.
Worthy Telemachus next outlined his
  plan of disposal:
'Death by the sword is too good for these sluts who
  brought to this household
shameful dishonour and sully us by their
  wanton cavortings.'
Seizing a hawser, removed from the deck of some
  blue-prowed vessel,
ever-resourceful Telemachus lashed it
  high on a column,
slung it across the dome of the outhouse,
  tautened it so that
anyone strung from it wouldn't be able to
  reach for a foothold.
Then, in the same way as thrushes or doves dropping
  into a thicket,
seeking a roosting-place, find only snares set
  cruelly to kill them,
so did the women, their heads in a row of
  tightly-drawn nooses,
dangle and writhingly twitch until death had
  stilled their convulsions.

Next, through the gate they dragged the treacherous
goatherd Melanthius
[trussed, he had been, by the hands and feet and
roped to a roof-beam,
left there suspended and suffering since the
heat of the battle].
Plying a keen-edged blade, they sawed his
nose and his ears off,
carved off his genitals, tossed them aside as
meat for the mongrels.
Finally, hacking his hands and his feet off, their
fury was sated.

Fates of Men

Many children are fathered,   fondled by parents,
fostered, sent forth;   but Fate is impartial:

maybe a man dies   mauled in his youth
by wandering wolves,   the wily heath-dwellers;
for some folk, famine   finishes all things;
hurricanes hurl   much hardship on one man;
ash-spears may bloody him;   the battlefield fell him;
one may go blundering,   blindness afflicting him;
another is lamed,   his leg's bones sundered
so that he moans,   menaced by Fate's lot,
one, forced to wander,   wearies of foreigners –
few men befriend him,   fearing his strangeness;
justice demands   the gibbet for one man,
then ravens visit him,   his viscera feed them;
the fierceness of fire   finishes many;
one man at his mead,   mouthing imprudently,
falls in a brawl,   a bright blade quietens him;
one, of a surfeit   supped at the beer-benches,
ends life in misery,   mindless, a self-slayer;
one man is fortunate,   finds joy early,
the company of kinsmen   comforts his dotage.

Thus men are ruled   by a random Weird:

one is regaled   with riches and youthfulness;
one, a warrior,   on the war-field is honoured;
one at the gaming-board   gains a great fortune;
a scholar is wealthy   in wisdom and intellect;
one is gifted   in the goldsmith's art,
adorns the corslet   of a king who gratefully
rewards him richly   with realms of his own;
one brews liquor   to lighten men's burden –
is hailed as a hero   and highly respected;
one procures patronage   plundering the word-hoard,
his skill in singing   is sought-after, paid for;
one becomes famed   as a falconer, taming
the wild hawk's spirit,   he speaks to it, feeds it,
its foot in a jess,   it gently succumbs...

Divers are the destinies   dealt out by Fate to us.

Ovidian

Aeolus stilled the winds, and the dawn star
  rose up refulgent
ushering mortals to get to their business.
  Perseus, rising,
put on his swift-winged sandals and with his
  hooked sword ascended,
cleaving the clear air, leaving behind him
  numerous nations,
coming at last to Cepheus' kingdom.
  Here was Andromeda,
unjustly fettered to pay for the heinous
  crime of her mother
[Cassiopeia (Cepheus' wife) had
  angered Neptune,
boasting herself more beautiful than his
  Nereid maidens].

Perseus saw her, chain-bound there to the
sea-battered cliff-face,
would have assumed her an alabaster
monument, but that
hair from her forehead stirred in the wind and
tears from her eyes welled.
Then he fell deeply besotted in love with her,
stunned by her beauty –
almost forgetting to ply his heels' pinions,
such was his wonder.
Landing, he cried: 'You shouldn't be bound in
chains made of metal;
rather, the links that bond lovers should be
yours.' And he asked her
what was her name and her nation, and the
reason she suffered.
Being a virgin, she wouldn't presume to
speak to a stranger,
modestly would have hidden her face in her
hands, had they been free.
Freely, however, her eyes shed tears as
Perseus persisted.
Then, lest her silence might seem to imply some
culpable conduct,
hapless Andromeda told him her name and
that of her nation,
how she was fettered unjustly for the
crime of her mother,
there to endure an ocean monster's
molestations.

While she was speaking the waters roared and,
breasting the broad waves,
out of the dolorous deep advanced a
menacing ogre.
Shrilly she screamed. Her father and mother
(more so the latter)
each felt an impotent wretchedness, only
able to wail grief,
clinging the while to the chained girl, making
loud lamentations.

Perseus then addressed them: 'The time for
grief is unending;
time for actively helping, however, is
dreadfully short-lived.
If I were now to tell you that I am
Perseus, son of
Danae and Jupiter, Perseus who slew the
serpent-haired Gorgon,
Perseus who dared to brave the winds on
feathery pinions,
then I should prove myself eligible to
marry your daughter.
If I now add to these credentials
that of my service
(should the gods favour me), surely you'll have to
give me your blessing.'
This they agreed (in addition, a dowry) –
who could refuse it?

Then, as the beak of a galley, driven
hard by her oarsmen,
furrows the foam, so the monster's sternum
parted the water.
Now it was only a stone's throw from where they
stood at the cliff-base.
Suddenly Perseus sprung from the earth, rose
up to the high clouds.
Seeing his shadow traversing the sea, the
monster attacked it.
Just as an eagle, sighting a basking
snake in a sunned field,
stoops on the scaled neck, deeply embedding
dagger-sharp talons
lest the infuriated reptile
twists its fangs backwards,
so, swooping swiftly, Perseus burst through the
air in a steep dive,
buried his sword to the hilt in the monster's
bellowing body.
Goaded, enraged by the wound, the brute thrashed
rearing and plunging,
spinning around like the fierce wild boar when
baying hounds bait it.

Deftly avoiding the greedily snapping
   maw of the monster,
plying his pinions, the hero struck its
   barnacled hump-back,
thrusting his curved blade deep in its ribs and
   slashing the finned tail.
Spray from the gushes of purple vomit
   spewed by the monster
spattered the wings of Perseus, made them
   heavy with blood spume.
Fearing to trust these gore-drenched pinions
   further, the hero
reached for a rock projecting above the
   wind-lashed surface.
Bracing himself, he firmly gripped this
   crag with his left hand,
thrusting his blade with his right hand repeatedly
   into the beast's guts –
Olympus itself, as well as the common
   people, applauded.

Cassiopeia and Cepheus, joyous,
   lauded the hero,
calling him son-in-law, saying he'd saved their
   house from destruction.
Unchained, the reason/reward for this feat of
   daring descended;
meanwhile the victor cleansed his hands in the
   brine which they brought him.
So that Medusa's snake-haired head might
   suffer no damage,
thickly he laid down leaves on the ground and
   over them seaweed,
placing the head of the Gorgon on top of them.
   Living, absorbent,
freshly-gathered, the seaweed fronds turned
   stony and brittle –
just as today all corals retain this
   quality, pliant
under the water but petrifying when
   brought to the surface.

Perseus then built altars of turf to
honour three godheads:
one to Minerva, on which a cow was
sacrificed duly;
next he dispatched a calf in homage to
wing-footed Mercury;
finally, slaying a bull, he elicited
Jupiter's favour.
Claiming Andromeda now as his prize for so
worthy an exploit,
Perseus sought no more dowry, but straightway
moved to the feast where
Cupid and Hymen presided fuelling
fires with rich incense.
Garlands festooned the roof-tree; joyful
harps and flutes sounded;
huge folding doors flung back to reveal a great
golden interior;
sumptuous then was the banquet laid for
Cepheus' courtiers.

When it was finished and all had indulged in
Bacchic cavortings,
Perseus asked his hosts about local
customs and manners.
One of them answered him, adding: 'Now tell us,
valiant Perseus,
how you beheaded the Gorgon Medusa.' The
hero explained how
under cold Atlas there was a place whose
entrance was guarded
closely by two hag sisters who shared one
eyeball between them;
while it was being transferred from one to the
other, he stole it,
then travelled far through trackless rock-strewn
forests, arriving
finally where the Gorgons dwelt – on
all sides around him,
petrified beasts and men, all changed by
glimpsing Medusa.

He hadn't looked direct in her face but had
   rather observed her
safely by way of the image reflected
   bright in his bronze shield.
She and her snakes were asleep when he severed her
   head from her shoulders;
fleet-winged Pegasus and his brother were
   born from her spilt blood.

Further, the hero told of more dangers
   bravely encountered:
oceans and lands he had witnessed, even
   stars he had soared to,
bold on his beating wings. When he had finished,
   still they were eager –
one of his hearers asked why, of all the
   Gorgon sisters,
only Medusa had tresses of coiling
   hideous serpents.
'Since what you ask is of interest to all men,
   I will inform you.
She was once famed for her loveliness, sought by
   passionate suitors,
fairest of all her attributes was her
   hair (I was told this
thing by a man I once met who claimed to have
   seen her in those days).
Neptune, however, ravished the maid in
   Minerva's temple,
whereupon modest Minerva hid her
   face with her aegis,
punished the Gorgon by changing her locks to these
   writhing reptiles.
Now, on her corslet, Minerva still wears the
   likeness of serpents;
still, on the goddess's breastplate are etched these
   terrible emblems.'

Submission

Woken by intermittent gentle
punch-like sensation left of sternum.
Fleeting consideration of summoning
medical aid rejected (incurious
as to the Faculty's prognosis),
seeking instead to leave a cleared desk:
hasty addressing of this composed brief
final submission; inconsequentially
marking a page (Defoe on the Pestilence).

[...poor dispairing Creatures, who had the Distemper upon them, and were grown stupid, or melancholly by their Misery, as many were, wandred away into the Fields, and Woods, and into secret uncouth Places, almost any where to creep into a Bush, or Hedge, and DIE.]

Pestilential

The Country People adjacent do in Pity
carry them Food and set it at a Distance;
next Time they go, they find the Wretches dead,
the Food untouch'd.

Then they do dig a Hole
at a great Distance, then with long Poles and Hooks
drag the dead Bodys into the dug Pits,
coming to Wind-ward that the Bodys' Scents
might blow from them; and Many do go out thus.

*

Blind Piper was an ignorant weak poor Man
and walked his Rounds about 10 a Clock at Night
piping from Door to Door. Folk took him in
at Public Houses, plied him with Drink and Victuals
and sometimes Farthings; he in Return would pipe
and sing.

One Night, poor Fellow, in Coleman-street,
and having a Bellyfull, laid on a Wall
and fell a sleep, when Neighbours, seeing him thus,
and hearing the Bell Man, thought him but a Corse
and plac'd a Body truly dead beside him.
The Tumbrill took both Bodys up and shot them
into the Pit – tho' Piper was but drunk.

*

Soloman Eagle, an Enthusiast,
sallies abroad quite naked with a Pan
of burning Charcoal on his Head, denouncing
of Judgement upon the City; tho' he himself
is not at all infected, but in his Head.

Thucydidean

Continents then were affected by violent
earthquakes, eclipses,
withering droughts and subsequent famines,
pestilent outbreaks...
Faced with the Plague, the ignorant Faculty
shewed itself impotent;
equally useless were all of our sciences,
oracles, arts, prayers...
Burning sensations occurred in our heads, our
eyes became bloodshot,
inside our mouths there was bleeding from throat and
tongue, we grew breathless,

coughing and retching ensued, producing
   bile of all species,
genitals, fingers and toes became festered,
   diarrhoea burgeoned...

Terrible was the despair into which all
   fell when they realised
fully the weight and the magnitude of their
   diresome affliction...
Not enough living to bury the dead or
   cover the corpses...
Seeing how swift and abrupt were the changes
   Fortune allotted
(money and life alike being transient
   under the Pestilence),
profligate wretched citizens turned to
   lawless dishonour,
heedless of gods and of law for they thought themselves
   already sentenced –
then was there bloody and slaughterous civil
   mass insurrection.

St Laurence's

It used to be OK, indeed beneficial,
to sit for half-an-hour in April sun
on, say, the bench 'Placed here by Colonel Everett,
D.S.O./R.E., 1887
– 1963' but now it's not.

Only *naïfs* and reckless oldies loiter
(cataracts and skin-cancers burgeoning)
in the quiet precinct of St Laurence's.

Reiterative

[Churned out in '76,
the eroded, faded text...]

Cancel our dailies and monthlies:
population, energy, food,
delapse, kakistocracy,
alcoholism thriving...

For Western Industrial Man
this isn't just another
crisis but a climacteric...

This sot's liver – a metaphor
for currency's swollen decease
and Technological Man
and before him all *H. sap.*
and all that he can conceive
blown oversized by an ego
too big to survive itself
(what else, but dumbos like us,
could advocate 'More motor cars
to get us back on our feet'?)...

[A handful of weighed syllables
has no future (nor has Future).]

Nine out of ten oafs in the street,
a census informs us with cheer,
fondly imagine we'll find
deposits of copper and oil
ad nauseam, or find substitutes...
Meanwhile CIPEC and OPEC
won't *give* it away, we will pay –
or, atavistically, war...

As the Lifestyle Pages observe:
EARLY RETIREMENT IS COMING...

If ever the headlines strike home,
and they realise there's nothing to lose,
the nine out of ten will run riot –
like these on the Sports Page: terraces
dripping with apes' gore...

Yes,
add to the cumulate threats,
amassing at x to the nth,
bloody insurrection –
Homo erectus autophagous...

[That was in '76,
the hackneyed text is eroded,
somebody ain't been listening –
you, at the back, sit up
and fuckingwell pay attention.]

Alcmanic

[That which remains is incongruous; frail bond
palimpsest crumbling, with it the notion;
utterance utterly lost in hiatus;
all that remains is fragmentary:] *ear-ring*

Ovidian

[Perseus, freeing Andromeda from her
fetters, restored her
safe to the arms of her overjoyed father who
offered the hero
any reward he desired – and was answered: 'The
hand of your daughter.'
Cepheus consented (albeit she was al-
ready betrothed to
Phineus, her uncle). The marriage feast was
duly appointed...]

To the assembled guests in the royal
court of King Cepheus,
valiant Perseus was retailing deeds of
personal prowess.
Suddenly, raucous howls of a riot
rived the serene hall
(clearly no hymn to Hymen, but some
presage of mayhem),
as a calm sea is whipped by a squall to
furious breakers.

Phineus irrupted, leading the mob with a
bronze-pointed ash-spear
(out to avenge what he saw as the theft of his
promised Andromeda),
aimed it at Perseus, tensed for the throw, but
Cepheus held him:
'Brother, what madness impels you to this grave
criminal action?
It wasn't Perseus who stole your bride, but
malicious Neptune.
Perseus saved her from being molested;
you lacked the courage;
let him who rescued her marry her, for my
word has been given.'

Phineus glowered at his brother and then at his
rival, uncertain
which to attack. Then a violent spasm
gripped the aggressor –
harmless, his flung spear splintered the bench where
Perseus was seated.
Up leaped the hero, tugged the wedged weapon
loose and re-launched it.
Phineus dodged it, diving behind the
altar for cover.
Rhoetus, however, stood in the path of the
terrible javelin,
full in the face he was struck by the bronze spike,
sunk to the floor, felled;
when the cold metal was wrenched from his cloven
face-bones his heels drummed,
kicking convulsively, then the spread tables were
spattered with blood gouts.

Baying for spilt guts, the rest of the rabble
took up their weapons,
some of them yowling that Cepheus ought to
perish with Phineus –
Cepheus, however, had already left the
palace, invoking
Justice and Faith and the Gods of Hospi-
tality, saying
how he abhorred this outrage. Meanwhile,
bellicose Pallas
flew to the aid of Perseus with the
strength of her aegis.

There was an Indian, Athis, a handsome
youth of just sixteen,
rich robes enhancing his beauty, a gold chain
gracing his neck, his
ringlets, adorned with a golden headband,
perfumed with sweet myrrh –
Athis, renowned for hurling the javelin,
famed as an archer.
Now the boy bent his bow, Perseus seized a
brand from the altar,

swung the still-smouldering cudgel, smashed it
   into the lovely
features; the face was instantly splattered,
   pulped into flenched mash.
Athis' lover, Lycabas, when he
   saw the boy dying,
wept for the mangled youthfulness, paused and
   snatched up the strung bow:
'Now you have me to contend with, not for
   long will you triumph
over the death of a boy whose slaying
   does you no credit –
merely arouses contempt.' And the arrow
   sped from the bowstring.
Missing its target, it lodged in the sleeve of
   Perseus' garment.
Then the great hero wielded his falchion
   (that which had severed
Gorgon Medusa's hideous head) and
   lunged into Lycabas.
Lycabas, moribund, crawled to the place where
   Athis' body
lay, and he fell there, soon to expire with
   this consolation:
even in death there is comfort through sharing,
   joined with a loved friend.

Two more, Phorbas and Amphimedon, were
   eager to join in,
slipped on the blood that flooded the floor and
   slid in the offal.
As they attempted to regain their balance
   Perseus was at them,
thrust his curved blade through the ribcage of one and the
   throat of the other.

Eurytus came next, wielding a lethal
   two-bladed battleaxe.
Perseus dispatched him by lifting a massive
   amphora (ornate,
richly embossed) and crashing it heavily
   on his opponent –

Eurytus spewed blood, fell on his back and,
agonised, twitching,
beat his smashed head on the smirched floor. Then in
rapid succession
Perseus slaughtered royal Polydaemon,
Abaris, Clytus,
Lycetus, Phlegyas, Helices... all the while
trampling corpses.

Phineus didn't dare tackle his foe in
hand-to-hand combat.
Hurling his spear, he missed and struck Idas
(who, until now, had
sided with nobody). Idas tugged out the
javelin, snarling:
'Phineus, you force me to face you in conflict;
you shall pay dearly.'
He was about to heave back the weapon when
loss of blood felled him.

Hodites then was carved up by Clymenus,
Hypseus struck down
Prothoenor, and Hypseus in turn was
butchered by Perseus...

There was an old man, Emathion, who was
just and god-fearing –
age kept him out of the fray, but his sharp tongue
served as a weapon.
Now he stepped forward and called down a curse on
causeless aggression.
As he was clinging with trembling hands to the
altar, a sword-stroke
wielded by Chromis sliced off his head which
fell on the altar,
there to exhale its last in the altar-fire,
still execrating.

Then the twin brothers, Broteas and Ammon,
consummate boxers
(boxing-gloves, though, are no match against cold steel),
fell to cruel Phineus;
likewise Ampycus, a priest of Ceres.

Standing aside was
hapless Lampetides, poet/musician,
there for the wedding,
nervously plucking his harp-strings – the sound was
heard by Petalus:
'Go sing the rest of your dirge to the ghosts in
Hades!' he taunted,
driving his sword through the dome of the useless
poet's left temple.
Groaning and twanging discordantly, he went
down in a welter.

Irate Lycormas, avenging this outrage,
ripped out a door-jamb,
smashed it down onto the neck of Petalus (who
sunk like a slain bull).

One called Pelates was trying to wrench the
jamb from the other
side, when his palm was pinned to the post by
Corythus' flung spear,
so that he hung by his hand without falling
when Abas slew him.

Melanus, too, a supporter of Perseus,
died. Then Dorylas,
one of the wealthiest landowners ever,
suffered obscenely
when he was speared through the testicles, and his
callous assailant
commented: 'This, where you lie, is the only
land you'll be left with.'

Perseus then, to redress this foul slaughter,
snatched out the shaft (still
warm with the blood of Dorylas) and loosed it
back at its owner –
in through his nose it thwacked, out through his neckbone.

Favoured by fortune,
Perseus next slew a couple of brothers,
Clytius and Clanis
(born of one mother – died of two different wounds):

Clytius fell when
both of his thighs were skewered by Perseus'
lethal flung ash-shaft;
Clanis expired with a spear down his throat, teeth
clenched on the cold spike.

Celadon, Astreus, Aethion (this last
noted for being
skilled in clairvoyance – albeit he failed to
forecast his own end),
also Thoactes and infamous parri-
cidal Agyrtes...
all of these fell by the spear or the blade of the
bloodthirsty hero.

Still there remained more gratuitous violence
on the agenda.
All the attackers were set to get Perseus,
ganged up against him,
failed to acknowledge his valour, openly
countered the king's pledge.
Cepheus' wife and Andromeda filled the
hall with their shrieking
protests against this atrocity, but their
outcries were drowned by
clashing of sword-blades and spear-tips and groans of
agonised dying.
(All the while, blood-loving loathsome Bellona,
goddess of warfare,
stirred up new trouble, defiling with gore the
peace of the household.)

Phineus and his thousand supporters
swarmed about Perseus.
Javelins flew either side of the hero
thicker than hailstones.
Setting his back to a massive stone column he
faced the mob's onslaught.
Molpeus led from the left and Ethemon
rushed on the right flank.
Molpeus he stopped with a slash through the leg, then
turned his attention

in the direction of frenzied Ethemon who
thrust his sword wildly,
hoping to sink it in Perseus' neck but he
struck the stone column.
Shattered, the steel bounced back at Ethemon and
stuck in his own throat.
As he stood trembling, suppliant, Perseus
ran his blade through him.

Finally, Perseus acknowledged that he was
grossly outnumbered:
'Now you have forced me to summon the help of the
Gorgon Medusa –
anyone here who is friendly towards me,
now is the time to
quickly avert your eyes.' Saying which, he raised
high the appalling
head of the Gorgon. Sceptical Thescalus
shouldered his javelin:
'Find someone else to intimidate with your
magical nonsense...'
but, as he braced to launch the shaft, he was
petrified, static.

Ampyx came next, but his sword-thrust at Perseus
halted in mid-stroke.
Nileus leaped forward proclaiming his greatness,
threatening Perseus –
suddenly he was cut off in mid-speech, his
open lips silenced.
Whereupon Eryx upbraided the warriors:
'It's your own cowardice,
not any mystical power of a hag's head,
makes you stand rigid!
Rush in with me and we'll overthrow this rash
youth and his magic!'
As he raced forward he turned to a statue,
clad in cold granite.

These all deserved the fate meted out by the
hero; however,
one called Aconteus, Perseus' ally,
fighting for his cause,

chanced to catch sight of the Gorgon and instantly
froze into marble.
Thinking him still to be living, Astyages
struck with his long sword
only to hear the steel echoing shrilly
off the stone statue;
standing amazed, he himself was transformed to
stone in a moment.

So many perished that listing them would be
too time-consuming.
Only two hundred survivors remained when
fighting had finished;
two hundred more glimpsed the head of the Gorgon and
turned into cold stone.

Finally, Phineus regretted the conflict
which he had started.
Seeing his statuesque forces fixed in
various postures,
wildly he called them, touched them, incredulous
that they were marble.
Turning away in confession of failure,
suppliant Phineus
cried out to Perseus pleadingly, begging:
'You are the victor!
Hide it away, that petrifying
head of Medusa.
It wasn't hate or ambition that made me
bear arms against you.
Why I made war was because of the woman
I was betrothed to –
you had done more to deserve her, but I had
known her for longer.
I am content to yield, grant me just one thing,
greatest of heroes,
only my life.' As he babbled this plea, he
didn't dare look up.
'Cowardly Phineus,' Perseus riposted,
'do not be fearful.
What I can give you, I will, and don't worry,
no sword shall hurt you.

I'll even make you a lasting memorial
   here in this palace,
so that my wife may be comforted by the
   sight of her suitor.'

Saying which, Perseus brandished the head of the
   hideous Gorgon
right in the face of the fear-stricken Phineus
   so that he saw it –
tears on his cheeks turned to stone and the craven
   cringing expression,
captured in marble, was permanent, petrified,
   pleading for mercy.

Fragmentary

felled by Fate,   this fine-wrought wall.
...castle is crumbled,   constructed by giants.
Rooftrees are wrecked,   ruined towers
fester and fall.   Fate fells all.
What of the craftsmen?   Clasped in earth.
In the grave's grasp   great men perish.
Grey lichen grows   on the gore-stained stone,
the gate is mouldered,   masons of genius
bound with iron   the base of the wall...
buildings abounded,   bath-houses, dwellings,
mead-halls were many   where men would boast,
but all was felled   by Fate's onslaught.
Pestilence came,   killing abundantly.
Those men who might   have re-made it lay dead.
What was once fought for   is wasteland now.
These courts have become   coldly bereft;
ripped from the rooftrees,   wrecked tiles lie.
...once, many men   in moods of confidence,
girt in gold,   the gear of warriors,
flushed with wine,   wealthy in silver,
counted their prized   possessions jealously...

Stonework stood here,   a spa of water
gushed forth hotly…

                                [Hiatus, lacuna…
as the city is sunken   so is the word-hoard,
faded the fragile   fragment of manuscript,
parchment eroded   round the sad utterance.]

Shard

As on a shard of Athenian amphora,
   summer remains fixed:
under a vine an impassioned Bacchic
   acolyte kisses,
squirting a jet of Riesling from his mouth
   into his lover's…

Winter: the wizened clusters cling to a
   frosted tendril,
fructose is concentrated, a honeyed
   vinous mnemonic…

Only one line remains of an antique
   lyrist's burden:
Sweet wine passes between the lips of
   amative partners…

Midnight,

a hotel bedroom, open window,
sibilant tyres on rain-washed asphalt streets
whispering a repetitious *finish, finish.*
You stroke your lover comprehensively,
who purrs contentment, clings to your neck and sobs.
Sibilant tyres on rain-washed asphalt streets
whispering a repetitious *finish, finish.*

[Untitled]

A silver ear-ring,
lost last night in the hayfield,
lies in flattened grass.

Exilic

From a lifetime of loss   this lament is compounded.
Since girlhood, no greater   grief has befallen me:
daily to suffer   the sorrow of exile,
leagues from my lover   in a land inaccessible.
Each dawn is desolate,   I desire him nightly.
Seas separate us,   sundered, I yearn for him.
Only death should divide us –   we drank to that often,
but all is altered.   Alien feelings
that he no longer   loves me as formerly
fill me with fear,   forlornly I pine here.
Lucky ones lie   lovingly together
in bed until morning;   myself, lonely,
in a fell forest   you'll find my earth-lair.
Here sobbing I sit   through summer, exiled.
Far from its haven,   my heart is storm-lashed.

Valedictory

This buffer's in full retreat,
had more than enough, wants out,
can't hack the hassle, the horseshit,
the bozos on mountain bikes,
the user-hostile high-tech,
the esoteric subculture
where 'The Gorgs plant binoony berries
which the Fraggles just can't stand!',
where 'T-Bag meets Dr Strangebag
and rapidly goes off fish!',
where each successive bulletin
is more wacky, sad, obscene...
This buffer's had more than enough,
wants out, is in full retreat.

Idyllic

Chambré, decanted, '34 port (Tuke
   Holdsworth) – the stopper
carefully sealed for conveying by rucksack
   into an idyll.

[Two bushes grafted together, olive with
   wild oleaster,
through which the rain-laden wind could never
   penetrate coldly,
nor did the sun ever pierce them with shafts of
   radiant noon heat.
Crawling beneath them he gathered together a
   litter of leafmould,
lay down at last in the midst of the leaves and
   piled them around him.

Whereat Athene covered his eyelids,
   soon to release him
out of his weary exhaustion, benignly
   easing with sweet sleep.]

Thirty secured in a little brown bottle
   after a month of
(bogus insomnia) locum's prescriptions,
   comforting rattle...

Distant a fortnight (a farmer's *frisson*,
   finding corrupt flesh),
distant a valley (nearest point of
   vehicular access),

kingfisher-blue pulsating strobe and
   bray of the tumbril.

August:

                    the steady thresh
of an advancing harvester;
the dark swift departing;
ash in Ludlow church,
HIC IACET A.E.H.;
last light is pressing the panes;
lcs lauricrs sont coupés.

Eh OS IvE

crackle   of brittle

anhydr   us laurel leaves

rustle of old

wizened anhydr .tous scrivenings,

frail wisps of laurel

half-hidden,   leaves,

glimpsed sorrowful

parchment er   utterance

and the sad utterance

sepia faded

pages of fadelous holograph

sepia-scrivenapsest hieroglyphs

rotted the frail mbled eroded leaves

bond, with it the

utterance

,

Nothing For Anyone

Cancel our Dailies and Monthlies.

Population, Energy, Food
The present United Nations
Forecast of Population
for year 2000 is over
7000 millions.
[illegible] spells it out for us*
(Encounter, March [illegible])
for Western Industrial Man
[illegible] just [illegible]
crisis but a climacteric.

[illegible] weighs a Sunday Sup.
[illegible] of alcoholism

The Art correspondent, clearly,
don't know his Art from his Albert.

In [illegible] sex, I read, there are more
[illegible] per square stock broker's
[illegible] than anywhere [illegible]

The sot's liver + a metaphor
[illegible] sterling's swollen decease
and technological Man
and before him Roman, Mayan,
Minoan, all homo erectus
[illegible] he conceives as [illegible]
in his [illegible] perspective
blown oversize by an ego
too big to survive itself.
(What [illegible] dummies like us
could air [illegible] 'More motor cars
to put us back on our feet'?)

* A Second Look at Doom, by [illegible] Ashby [illegible] Encounter, Vol XLVI No. 3

Som • sn velling Calf reviews verse.
Compared with De Witts Black Holes,*
... all ... weighed ... ll les
... future (nor has future).
... ONE HUNDRED TODAY,
... ES HIS FITNESS TO ...
LIFE-DRUG KNOWN ONLY TO HIM!
(C... ... nde ... Ferret ...
in ... nc... let's *Lancet* *Graves*
'... this rare Elixir of Long Life,
if p... per... used, will protract
your days till you shall have seen
...ur count...

Of course
it will ... take us by surprise –
...ne ... in the street,
...ens... ...m... with cheer,
... will find
deposit... ...oper and oil
ad... ...r ...s ... ...tures.
Pos... ... possibly not. –
Meanwhile, ...IPE... and C...
won't *give* ... away, we will ... y –
t... ...avistically;

As ... Leisure Pages observ...
EAR... RE... ...
... o8vu... snt...c ... u
... pcɔlq ... lliv ... ...
... ...t ot ... ...
...eta, ...
... 'sɘ ... ...

Black Holes, ed... ee by Cecile De Witt and ... S. De Witt
Breach, ...

...io virgil p.c.
Frankly we ... ... lese

ESCHATOLOGICAL

(1996)

Choric

There is no thing in the archive of angry
heaven – affliction,
terror, distress – but unfortunate man must
bear the weight of it.

FROM *Beowulf*

In the barrow were buried   the brightest of jewels,
treasures (concealed   in the kists) from an ancient
nation of nobles   now long extinct,
of whom one sole   survivor remained
guarding the garner,   greeting his kinsmen
(whose fate, he was sure,   he'd share before long –
that of possessing   the plunder but briefly).
Newly built on a coast-cliff   and close to hand,
reinforced to repel   any raiders, the tumulus
had served the lone guardian   to secrete the trove.
He addressed the hoard,   hear what he uttered:

Ground, now grasp   what great men couldn't –
earls'-wealth won   by warriors long ago.
Horrors of battle   bereft me of kinsfolk
with each of whom   in the Hall I shared feasting.
Who will wield this brand   now brave men are gone?
Or burnish to brightness   this bowl and drinking cup?
Brave men are gone...   this gold-tempered helmet
is destined to shed   its shining adornment.
Those who furbished to brilliance   the battle-mask sleep now.
Armour, once forged   to fend off the swords'-crash
where the shields clashed   and shattered in battle,
now, with the warrior,   is wasted debris.
This chain-mail corslet   can't journey far
when the one who bore it   to battle is absent.
No *scop* tunes the harp   to sharpen our gladness,
no prized hawk flies   from the fist through the Hall,
there is no swift steed   to stamp in the courtyard.
A great death has direfully   dealt with the living.

Thus lamenting, lachrymose,   the lone survivor
went night and day   till death stroked his heart.

I.M., G.E.

Gavin Buchanan Ewart has left us
wiser but sadder;
Putney and Parnassus grieve –
I drink and fiddle with verse.

Choric

You do not know yet, O unhappy man, what
evils await you:
open these leaves and observe
weltering corpses, and worse.

Life will afford few happy events to
man, though a thousand
various woes will conspire,
wearing and weighing him down.

Throned on Olympus, Zeus unexpectedly
nods, and our hopes fail.

Leasts

This is a shoddy compromise: Muscle
   Beach and the big boys;
grudgingly granted the only unwanted
   space, a barbed kampong
(somewhat resembling that in which Nippon
   hosted the Old Chap)
wherein a few remaining Least Terns
   hack an existence.

Exilic

Wulf on one island,   I waste on another
in exile; a foul   fen separates us.
I waste, weeping   for my Wulf in the rain's-drench,
weakened by wanting him.   Wulf, we are sundered.

Corporate

In polystyrene, snug sarcophagi,
corporate burgers (each in uniform
coat of congealed bright ketchup) are served up
by a drum-majorette with *Hi! I'm Sharon*
emblazoned on a badge close to her heart.

*

Flunkeys and bell-hops (pawns of Corporate
Imagery con-men) slyly multiply.
Handcuffs and truncheons burgeon, wielded by
bullethead bullnecks, quondam night-club bouncers,
ex-SAS with homicidal skills,
lager-louts, dandy privatised militia.

*

Garbage-men clad in incandescent pink
testify to our Nation's Corporate
Success – seldom has shit been shunted round
with such decorum, pageantry and pomp.

*

Furled brolly, dandruffed pinstripe, slimline briefcase,
on Friday nights give way to leisure mufti –
trainers and Levi's, golfing garb and Barbour,
green wellies…
All too soon Monday's commuter
resumes the swindling, sartorial City.

*

Quite probably the last things we shall see
are the starched yashmak of the Trust Fund surgeon
and dapper paramedics dressed to kill.

Choric

Those to whom mortal life is bestowed and who
live it serenely,
free from the blows of affliction, must be con-
sidered the blessèd.

Lucretian

I

When men were oppressed by the gods,
   scared shitless by superstition,
Epicurus, empiricist hero,
   first took a cool look at religion,
boldly concluded, 'Balderdash!'
   He wasn't impressed by the twaddle
of sky-pilots – thunder and lightning,
   he knew, was Physics not Zeus.
In his mind he meandered the cosmos,
   came back triumphant to tell us
what can and can not exist,
   and the limits of natural phenomena.
So he trampled the trite old trash
   underfoot, and raised our status.

Religio-magico-malice –
   remember the slaughter at Aulis
when innocent Iphigeneia
   was sacrificed by her own father,
deluded devout Agamemnon,
   who thought that to summon a breeze
which would speed his fleet to Troy
   he must first placate bloodthirsty Artemis
with a welter of gore and guts
   and the mumbo-jumbo and cleavers
of a pack of murderous priests...
   (Remember, also, Khomeini
and Tomás de Torquemada.)
   How much idiot evil
gormless theists engender.

II

Each organism achieves
its acme of growth then declines,
the vigour and strength of its prime
slipping to age and decay –
copious ingestion of food
cannot keep pace with the surge
of fecal exudation.
Every thing ends when its innards
ebb and it cedes to the blows
with which it's assailed from without.

So do the walls of the world
presently start to implode.
Earth, which engendered so much,
is unable, now, to support us,
possessed of more shit than nutriment.
Ploughs are eroded, the ploughmen
whinge that they've wasted their time,
envy the farms of their forbears
whose smallholdings yielded more bushels
per hectare than any do now.
Worldlings are loath to acknowledge
that their planet, like all other bodies,
is subject to senile attrition.

III

[Only pain, not oblivion, hurts.]
Since the mind, like the body, is mortal,
death doesn't matter a toss.
When the brain and the carcass are severed,
we, who shall then be nothing,
can be troubled by nothing at all.

If we have ever existed
in any previous state,
we *now* know nothing about it;
so, when we snuff it, we won't
feel deprived of the present.

If, after death, there were dearth,
then the mind would have to be present
to experience deprivation;
but death, which denies the existence
of thought, exempts us from this.

One who no longer *is*
can't suffer – is merely the same
as one who has never been.

In sleep, neither mind nor body
feels itself 'absent' or craves life.
Extend this repose to eternity –
no sense of loss can obtain.

Prolonging life doesn't reduce
the duration of death, for the time
after departure is infinite –
non-being lasts just as long
for those who expire today
as it does for defunct Eolithics.

IV

When a man is afflicted by Venus
he soon surrenders his sanity.
If he nurtures the amative urge,
daily his lunacy deepens.
His only cure is diversion
from the single cause of his madness:
he must cultivate many cathartic
promiscuous petty liaisons
and random ejaculations –
otherwise, aimless, bewildered,
he neglects his professional duties,
his reputation is ruined,
his strength is sapped and his living
is ruled by the whim of a woman
who soon wastes his wealth on perfumes,
gewgaws from Babylon, Sicyon,
raiments from Malta and Cos,
then flutters her eyes at some other
gullible hapless twerp.

This madness is frequently manifest
  in the terms of endearment employed
by the crazed one towards his beloved:
  thus slatterns and slags are 'enchantresses';
the beanpole is 'lithe as an antelope';
  the dwarfish scrubber, 'petite';
the massive-papped slob, 'statuesque';
  the eldritch harridan rates as
'a great conversationist'...
  But, even supposing the subject
were Aphrodite incarnate,
  the facts remain: there *are* others,
we managed without her before,
  and the filth of bodily functions
is the same in the slut as the sylph.

V

  Consider earth, ocean and sky,
matter so diverse in nature –
  all, in one day, will expire.
Our planet, its structure and substance,
  4,600 million
years old, in a day will collapse.

  You may well be hapless enough
to have to give credence to this
  through your own particular witness –
let us hope not though, may common sense
  convince you of this dread certainty.

Don't think for a moment (fettered
  by superstition) that stars,
earth, sea, sky and moon
  are immortal, divinely endowed –
they ain't. And don't think, either,
  that 'the gods' created this world
so that we ought to praise it,
  never calling to question
its nature and degeneration.
  What could immortals gain
from devotion by wimps like us?
  What would it matter to us
if we'd never been created?

Perhaps, though, it's understandable
that, when the whole planet shudders
and cities totter and crumble,
mortals create self-doubtings
and lapse and contrive their divinities.

VI

fatal the spread of the pestilence
laying the whole of them low
foreheads grotesquely distended
saline green phlegm from their throats
putrid black blood through bolocked nostrils
blindness limbs stiffened in death
penises rotted to stumps
vultures repulsed by their stench
city and country vile heaps
bile slime cadavers piles stink
filth-smirched in rags without homes
loathsome the sores and the shite
carcasses foulness pus oozed
groaning unquenchable mad

Choric

Why is there silence in front of the household?
   No friend to tell us.

Not even minions remain to report the
   violent débâcle.

Deeply the groans burst from him that has lost his
   home and his fortune,
roof-tree and cooking-hearth sacked and his wife and
   family sundered.

Randomly fates are dispensed to us by the
   gods: at one moment
blessings are showered on us which our hopes had
   dared not aspire to;
next are apportioned us various ills such as
   these which assail us
(such is the outcome of this happy day which
   destiny deals us).

Have you, in readiness, made preparation for
   adequate sadness?

News

Nothing, fond parent attempting to shield your
   child from the onslaughts
waged by quotidian strife (we observe you
   on tonight's shitshow
try, with a frail and futile attempt at
   resuscitation),
      can counter the cunts with the creeds,
      barriers, borders, beliefs.

[Untitled]

Cranium cracked;   corrupt limbs;
gape sags;   slack thews;
neck gnawed;   knuckles and foot-bones
mangled; maggots   mumble between ribs,
gore and gristle   they guzzle from the corpse,
in tatters they tear   the tongue for a feast
(silencing wit   and wise erudition),
eat out the eyes   of the ice-cold cadaver
which warmed itself once   with woolen garments.

Both poor men and wealthy   worry to think of this.

Epitaphal

Truculent? Maybe. Yet possessed of virtue
by being, albeit a shit, not garrulous.

*

You thought him cruel? No more than you should think
a Turkey Vulture cruel – vocations differ.

Choric

I don't *know*; but my mind presages ill.
   Observe the abhorrent and atrocious deeds
   done by their butcherous inhumanity.
Other horrors, other woes
rise and enwrap the beleagured house;
round the polluted altars, stains.
   Over rich rooms, once scenes of joy,
   horror and desolation reign.
For your ruined country, woe
(such is the pleasure of the gods)
succeeds to woe, and rabid dogs
infest the streets, and banks foreclose.
   Unhappy children, wasted is your city,
   your mothers, beyond succour, desolate.
Our sufferings are alike, we are reminded
by your grief of our own unhappy state.
   Can any curse severer be devised
   for mortals, than to see their children dead?
What plaints are these I hear? Who strike their breasts
uttering lamentations for the dead?
   Can there be deeds more horrible than these
   left for succeeding ages to produce?
O ruthless fate!
O unhappy land!
O mournful voice!
Oimoi!
   Alas! In quick succession across this land
   ill rolls on ill and raging flames spread ravage.
Loud cries and shrieks resound, tall towers are down,
fuliginous flames rise round them, Troy lies trashed.
   Our house is shaken by calamity,
   but we, with patience, must endure fate's onslaught.
I don't *know*; but my mind presages ill.

[Untitled]

earth shall heave   high hills fall
covers of graves   groan and melt
minds of men   be maddened by waves'-roar
sky grow dark   dim black chaos
extinguish stars   the sun fail
nor will lunar   light brighten
deathly tokens   terrify the wretched
atmosphere filled   with fire blazing
no man able   to abide its fury
kings and their people   poor and wealthy
together shall feel   fear equal in weight
flaming vapours   vicious ice
excess of heat   horror of cold
eyes shall weep   without cessation
agonised men   meander forever
void black night   no noises heard
but violent weeping   woe lamentation
nothing to be found   but foulness there
no scent there   but the stench of corruption
wailing lips   lambent with flame
and worms ravening   rending and gnawing
no ease or solace   solitary endurance
no help against hardship   horror unbearable
universal insanity   senility wrath
weariness indolence   insomnia earth shall

[No fatuity
of which *H. sap* can conceive
remains unfulfilled.]

INDEX OF TITLES & FIRST LINES

INDEX OF TITLES & FIRST LINES

(The prefix 1 refers to pages in volume 1 while 2 refers to volume 2; titles are shown in italics, first lines in roman type)